POPULATION AND LAND USE IN DEVELOPING COUNTRIES

REPORT OF A WORKSHOP

Carole L. Jolly and Barbara Boyle Torrey, Editors

Committee on Population
Commission on Behavioral and Social Sciences and Education
National Research Council

NATIONAL ACADEMY PRESS
Washington, D.C. 1993

National Academy Press • 2101 Constitution Avenue, N.W. • Washington, D.C. 20418

NOTICE: The project that is the subject of this report was approved by the Governing Board of the National Research Council, whose members are drawn from the councils of the National Academy of Sciences, the National Academy of Engineering, and the Institute of Medicine. The members of the committee responsible for the report were chosen for their special competences and with regard for appropriate balance.

This report has been reviewed by a group other than the authors according to procedures approved by a Report Review Committee consisting of members of the National Academy of Sciences, the National Academy of Engineering, and the Institute of Medicine.

The National Academy of Sciences is a private, nonprofit, self-perpetuating society of distinguished scholars engaged in scientific and engineering research, dedicated to the furtherance of science and technology and to their use for the general welfare. Upon the authority of the charter granted to it by the Congress in 1863, the Academy has a mandate that requires it to advise the federal government on scientific and technical matters. Dr. Bruce Alberts is president of the National Academy of Sciences.

The National Academy of Engineering was established in 1964, under the charter of the National Academy of Sciences, as a parallel organization of outstanding engineers. It is autonomous in its administration and in the selection of its members, sharing with the National Academy of Sciences the responsibility for advising the federal government. The National Academy of Engineering also sponsors engineering programs aimed at meeting national needs, encourages education and research, and recognizes the superior achievements of engineers. Dr. Robert M. White is president of the National Academy of Engineering.

The Institute of Medicine was established in 1970 by the National Academy of Sciences to secure the services of eminent members of appropriate professions in the examination of policy matters pertaining to the health of the public. The Institute acts under the responsibility given to the National Academy of Sciences by its congressional charter to be an adviser to the federal government and, upon its own initiative, to identify issues of medical care, research, and education. Dr. Kenneth I. Shine is president of the Institute of Medicine.

The National Research Council was organized by the National Academy of Sciences in 1916 to associate the broad community of science and technology with the Academy's purposes of furthering knowledge and advising the federal government. Functioning in accordance with general policies determined by the Academy, the Council has become the principal operating agency of both the National Academy of Sciences and the National Academy of Engineering in providing services to the government, the public, and the scientific and engineering communities. The Council is administered jointly by both Academies and the Institute of Medicine. Dr. Bruce Alberts and Dr. Robert M. White are chairman and vice chairman, respectively, of the National Research Council.

Library of Congress Catalog Card No. 93-86389
International Standard Book Number 0-309-04838-9

Additional copies of this report are available from: National Academy Press, 2101 Constitution Avenue, N.W., Box 285, Washington, D.C. 20055. Call 800-624-6242 or 202-334-3313 (in the Washington Metropolitan Area).

B059

Copyright 1993 by the National Academy of Sciences. All rights reserved.

Printed in the United States of America

COMMITTEE ON POPULATION

SAMUEL H. PRESTON (*Chair*), Population Studies Center, University of Pennsylvania
RONALD D. LEE (*Chair-elect*), Department of Demography, University of California, Berkeley
JOSE-LUIS BOBADILLA, World Bank, Washington, D.C.
JOHN B. CASTERLINE, Department of Sociology, Brown University
KENNETH H. HILL, Department of Population Dynamics, Johns Hopkins University
DEAN T. JAMISON, School of Public Health, University of California, Los Angeles
ANNE R. PEBLEY, The RAND Corporation, Santa Monica, California
RONALD R. RINDFUSS, Department of Sociology, University of North Carolina
T. PAUL SCHULTZ, Department of Economics, Yale University
SUSAN C.M. SCRIMSHAW, School of Public Health, University of California, Los Angeles
BETH J. SOLDO, Department of Demography, Georgetown University
MARTA TIENDA, Population Research Center, University of Chicago
BARBARA BOYLE TORREY, Population Reference Bureau, Washington, D.C.
JAMES TRUSSELL, Office of Population Research, Princeton University
AMY O. TSUI, Carolina Population Center, University of North Carolina, Chapel Hill

LINDA MARTIN, *Director**
BARNEY COHEN, *Research Associate*
SUSAN COKE, *Senior Project Assistant**
KAREN A. FOOTE, *Research Associate*
DIANE GOLDMAN, *Administrative Assistant***
JAMES N. GRIBBLE, *Program Officer*
CAROLE L. JOLLY, *Program Officer*
PAULA J. MELVILLE, *Senior Project Assistant*

---

*through June 1993
**through July 1992

WORKSHOP PARTICIPANTS

Presenters

BARBARA BOYLE TORREY[+] (*Chair*), Population Reference Bureau, Washington, D.C.
RICHARD BILSBORROW, Carolina Population Center, University of North Carolina, Chapel Hill
HANS BINSWANGER, World Bank, Washington, D.C.
BILLIE R. DEWALT, Center for Latin American Studies, and the Graduate School of Public and International Affairs, University of Pittsburgh
ROBERT E. EVENSON, Department of Economics, Yale University
UMA LELE, Food and Resource Economics Department, University of Florida
WOLFGANG LUTZ, Population and Sustainable Development Project, International Institute for Applied Systems Analysis, Laxenberg, Austria
MICHAEL MORTIMORE, University of Cambridge, England
THEODORE PANAYOTOU, Harvard Institute for International Development, and Department of Economics, Harvard University
STEWARD T.A. PICKETT, Institute of Ecosystem Studies, New York Botanical Garden, Millbrook, N.Y.
SAMUEL H. PRESTON[+], Population Studies Center, University of Pennsylvania
VERNON W. RUTTAN, Department of Agricultural and Applied Economics, University of Minnesota
BILLIE L. TURNER II, George Perkins Marsh Institute, Clark University
M. GORDON WOLMAN, Department of Geography and Environmental Engineering, Johns Hopkins University
ISAAK S. ZONNEVELD, International Institute of Aerial Survey and Earth Science, Enschede, The Netherlands

Other Participants and Paper Coauthors

BARBARA CRANE, Department of Population Planning and International Health, University of Michigan
MARIA CONCEPCION J. CRUZ
WILFRIDO CRUZ, World Bank, Washington, D.C.
RUTH DEFRIES, Department of Geography, University of Maryland
ALENE GELBARD, Population Reference Bureau, Washington, D.C.
SARAH L. HAMILTON, Center for Computational Sciences, University of Kentucky
EINAR HOLM, International Institute for Applied Systems Analysis

SERGEI IVANOV, Population Division, United Nations, New York
JEFF JORDAN, Population Resource Center, Princeton, N.J.
CAROLYN MAKINSON, Andrew W. Mellon Foundation, New York
MELANIE MARLETT, Office of Strategic Planning, Agency for
    International Development, Washington, D.C.
WILLIAM McGREEVEY, World Bank, Washington, D.C.
TOM MERRICK, World Bank, Washington, D.C.
TOM MORRIS, Office of Strategic Planning, Agency for International
    Development, Washington, D.C.
WILLIAM ROBERTSON, IV, Andrew W. Mellon Foundation, New York
J. BRAD SCHWARTZ, Center for International Development, Research
    Triangle Institute, Research Triangle Park, N.C.
ELLEN STARBIRD, Office of Population, Agency for International
    Development, Washington, D.C.
C. SHANNON STOKES, Department of Agricultural Economics and Rural
    Sociology, Pennsylvania State University
TERRY TIFFANY, Office of Population, Agency for International
    Development, Washington, D.C.
JAMES TRUSSELL,[+] Office of Population Research, Princeton University
MICHAEL VLASSOFF, Population Division, United Nations, New York
STEPHEN VOSTI, International Food Policy Research Institute,
    Washington, D.C.

National Research Council Staff

CARLA CARLSON, Board on Agriculture
E. WILLIAM COLGLAZIER, Office of International Affairs
ROB COPPOCK, Commission on Behavioral and Social Sciences and
    Education
DIANE GOLDMAN, Committee on Population
JAMES N. GRIBBLE, Committee on Population
CAROLE L. JOLLY, Committee on Population
LINDA G. MARTIN, Committee on Population
JOAN MONTGOMERY HALFORD, Committee on Population
JAMES REARDON-ANDERSON, Committee on Scholarly
    Communication with the People's Republic of China, Office of
    International Affairs
PAUL STERN, Committee on the Human Dimensions of Global Change
SUSANNE STOIBER, Division of Social and Economic Studies,
    Commission on Behavioral and Social Sciences and Education
JAMES TAVARES, Board on Agriculture

[+]Member, Committee on Population

Preface

This report summarizes the discussions and papers presented at a Committee on Population workshop on population growth and land use change in developing countries. The workshop, held December 5-6, 1991, at the National Academy of Sciences in Washington, D.C., brought together researchers from different disciplines to discuss recent research on the effects of population growth on land use.

In its 1986 report, *Population Growth and Economic Development: Policy Questions* (National Academy Press), the committee briefly considered the broad issue of population growth and the consequences for natural resources. With regard to land use, the report (National Research Council, 1986:33-34) concluded that "Rapid population growth poses two problems for agriculture. First, if no other conditions of production change, expansion of the agricultural labor force probably reduces labor productivity and correspondingly lowers agricultural wages. Second, population growth can accelerate the degradation of renewable resources. . . . The extent to which slower population growth would alleviate these problems depends on the degree to which the problems lead to other solutions through institutional and technological adaptation . . . if institutions do not adapt as rapidly as needed, slower population growth can retard the decline of labor productivity and the degradation of common resources."

In the 5 years that followed the publication of the report, public and policymaker interest in environmental issues continued to increase, and the committee decided to undertake another activity in this area. Instead of reviewing again a broad range of issues related to population and economic development, the committee developed a workshop on one aspect of the relationship in developing countries: population growth and land use change. The committee focused mainly on agrarian uses because of their important implications for agricultural production, soil quality, and climate change.

Approximately half of the workshop was devoted to general aspects of the topic: the history of land use change; the measurement of land use change; approaches to the study of population growth and land use; population-induced technological change in agriculture; the use of cross-national data to understand population and land use relationships; and institutional change. Because ecological, economic, demographic, and institutional conditions vary from place to place, the rest of the workshop focused on case studies. The case studies exhibited a variety of analytical strategies for studying the population and land use relationship. The agenda for the workshop is presented in the Appendix. Summary versions of some of the papers, chosen by the editors in consultation with members of the Committee on Population, are published in this report.

A summary of many of the themes of the workshop is contained in the Introduction. The themes represent the views of the individual workshop participants and do not necessarily cover all the important aspects of the population and land use relationship.

The committee wishes to thank the Office of Population of the U.S. Agency for International Development, the William and Flora Hewlett Foundation, and the Andrew W. Mellon Foundation, which generously provided the funding for the workshop. The committee also appreciates the efforts of the committee members who developed the workshop. Barbara Boyle Torrey chaired the workshop and devoted a great deal of energy and time to developing the meeting and preparing this report. James Trussell assisted in directing the workshop discussion.

The committee is also very grateful to M. Gordon Wolman, chair of the Commission on Geosciences, Environment, and Resources of the National Research Council, who provided valuable historical background about land use change and initiated much of the workshop discussion. We are also grateful to the other participants for their informed presentations and discussions. A planning meeting, at which topics for the workshop were identified, was attended by Richard Bilsborrow, Hans Binswanger, Steven Mink, Michael Philley, Samuel Preston, Scott Radloff, Ronald Ridker, Susanne Stoiber, and Barbara Boyle Torrey.

Finally, the committee would like to thank the National Research Council staff who assisted in this workshop. Carole L. Jolly had principal responsibility for the workshop and edited this report with Barbara Boyle Torrey. Linda G. Martin provided guidance on structuring the workshop as well as useful comments on earlier drafts of the report. Barney Cohen made helpful suggestions on improving the introduction and took care of unnumerable

PREFACE ix

details in the final drafting stages. Diane Goldman completed the logistical arrangements for the workshop, and Susan Coke prepared the papers for publication. Michael Edington copyedited, and Eugenia Grohman, Elaine McGarraugh, and Christine McShane, with Susan Coke, Paula Melville, and Kirsten Johnson, collaborated in the production of this report.

Samuel H. Preston, *Chair*
Committee on Population

Contents

1	Introduction *Carole L. Jolly and Barbara Boyle Torrey*	1
2	Population, Land Use, and Environment: A Long History *M. Gordon Wolman*	15
3	What Is Meant by Land Use Change? *Isaak S. Zonneveld*	30
4	An Ecological Perspective on Population Change and Land Use *Steward T.A. Pickett*	37
5	Northern Nigeria: Land Transformation Under Agricultural Intensification *Michael Mortimore*	42
6	India: Population Pressure, Technology, Infrastructure, Capital Formation, and Rural Incomes *Robert E. Evenson*	70
7	Mauritius: Population and Land Use *Wolfgang Lutz and Einar Holm*	98
8	Honduras: Population, Inequality, and Resource Destruction *Billie R. DeWalt, Susan C. Stonich, and Sarah L. Hamilton*	106
9	Population Growth, Environmental Change, and Innovation: Implications for Sustainable Growth in Agriculture *Vernon W. Ruttan*	124
	Appendix: Workshop Agenda	157

1

Introduction

Carole L. Jolly and Barbara Boyle Torrey

What are the effects of population growth on land use change? Despite the interest in and importance of this question, there is a relatively small body of carefully designed research that begins to provide answers to it. In order to make progress in this field we need to understand why careful research on this topic is so scarce, examine the work that has been done, and propose ways to encourage research in an area that may be critical to the future of many countries.

WHY THIS IS A DIFFICULT QUESTION TO ANSWER

One difficulty in developing general answers to the question posed is that much of the existing research has focused on case studies, in which results often depend on idiosyncracies of physical and human endowments. Consequently, although case studies are useful in illuminating particular intricacies of the population and land use relationship, they are not readily compared. In order for them to be comparable, a general framework of analysis would have to be developed and applied systematically to countries or areas in very different circumstances.

A second difficulty in studying the relationship between population growth and land use change is the challenge of precisely matching demographic and ecological data that generally are not collected over the same geographic regions. Demographic surveys are usually conducted by political region, such as a district or country; land use data are more often collected for a particular ecosystem or landscape, which can cross political boundaries. Even when demographic and land use data are gathered for the same area, no area is a closed system because migration complicates population dynamics and climate change complicates land use dynamics.

A third difficulty is that much of the research conducted on population growth and land use change has been weak in identifying and quantifying the set of causal connections between demographic and land use changes, making definitive conclusions difficult. Instead, much of the research has focused on documenting associations between land use changes and demographic variables rather than identifying the specific causes for particular changes.

Billie L. Turner highlighted several additional obstacles to research in this area in his presentation. He stressed that the data are very poor for global comparative studies of land use. Almost all land use data measure conversion of land to human use; there are few data on modification of land use. Other obstacles are the different views among social scientists about what constitutes proof of population and environment linkages. Finally, Turner noted that there is no agreement among scientists about the level of observation suitable for studying population and land use dynamics.

Research on population growth and land use change has been made more complicated by the use of two conflicting paradigms, one based in natural science (or classical economics) and the other in neoclassical economics. The natural science paradigm places more emphasis on the finiteness of resources than on technological and institutional change and the accumulation of physical and human capital. This paradigm views population growth as a threat to the inherent limits of arable land to provide food, shelter, and sustenance. The neoclassical economics paradigm emphasizes the accumulation of both physical and human capital and the substitution of abundant factors for scarce ones. This paradigm suggests that population growth can be the impetus for technological and other changes that mitigate or even eliminate the effects of natural resource limits on economic well-being. Empirical research is capable of indicating which of these paradigms has more explanatory power, but the research base is thin and has not yet led to a body of knowledge on which public or scientific consensus has developed.

Classical economists, beginning with Malthus, stressed the difficulty of maintaining a steady or increasing standard of living given a finite resource base and a growing population. Malthus argued that food production could only grow at a linear rate while populations grew geometrically; thus population growth would ultimately outstrip the ability of the economy to meet the demand for food (Malthus, 1798). Although agricultural production has so far met and often exceeded populations' growing needs for food, there remains a concern among many natural scientists that the ecological limits to food production provide little scope for future expansion (Ehrlich and Holdren, 1971; Ehrlich et al., 1977; Brown et al., 1991; Raven, 1991).

Much of the empirical research done under the natural science paradigm has focused on estimating carrying capacity to identify areas of population pressure. Research has also analyzed the effects of increasing human populations on species loss and ecoystems. A large study, undertaken by the Food and Agriculture Organization (FAO), analyzed the "population supporting capacities" of 117 developing countries and concluded that over half of the countries could not achieve food self-sufficiency by the year 2000 with low levels of inputs (mainly labor). Almost a third of the countries could not meet their needs even with an intermediate level of inputs (some fertilizer tools and simple conversation techniques). Nineteen countries could not meet their needs even at very high levels of inputs (advanced technology, complete mechanization, and all necessary conservation measures [Higgins et al., 1983]).

Neoclassical economists are also concerned with whether an economy can provide an increasing or steady standard of living given a finite resource base and a growing population. To determine whether output growth can keep up with population growth, attention is focused on two factors: technological advance and the substitution of scarce factors with more abundant ones (Stiglitz, 1979; Simon, 1981). Under well-functioning markets, as land resources become scarce, incentives will increase for people to develop technologies to farm previously unused land (extensification) and to increase production per existing unit of land (intensification). People will also substitute more abundant resources, such as fertilizer and labor, for land. In her widely cited work, Ester Boserup (1965, 1970, 1981) documented how, in response to greater population density, farmers reduced their fallow periods, began to use the plow, and implemented multiple cropping cycles to make their land more productive. Although she acknowledged that land degradation could occur as hills were cultivated or fallow periods excessively shortened, Boserup concluded that technology, such as terracing and fertilizer, could minimize the damage.

Under the neoclassical economics paradigm, land degradation can be the result of several factors, the most important being inefficient markets and lagged responses to population growth. For example, government subsidies have made it economically viable for people to settle the Amazon rain forest, where soil quality is poor and sustained agricultural production difficult (Schmink and Wood, 1987). Artificially low producer prices for agricultural products and lack of property rights in many countries in Africa have given farmers few incentives to conserve their land for future use (Lele and Stone, 1989). As populations increase and land resources become scarcer, farmers need to farm more intensively. But farmers and governments may not react quickly enough to develop technologies to farm their land more efficiently, resulting in land degradation.

THE INCREASING IMPORTANCE OF POPULATION GROWTH AND LAND USE CHANGE

The difficulty of doing research on this issue is commensurate with its increasing importance. The world's population is likely to double in the next 60 years, even if fertility rates fall in virtually every developing country (United Nations, 1991; World Bank, 1992; Bureau of the Census, 1991). This is because, regardless of how effective family planning programs may be in reducing fertility, the adult population of the next 20 years has already been born and its increased demand for food is inevitable. The earth's land resources will have to become more productive in the next 60 years if the growing needs for food are to be accommodated.

Today's population dynamics are unique. Although there is a negative correlation between density and natural increase (births minus deaths; see Table 1), many countries that are already very densely populated are still experiencing high rates of population growth (see Figures 1 and 2). Most of the research on population and land use change has focused on levels of population and population densities. However, rates of change in high-density countries may also be critical variables.

The increases in the world's population will not be evenly distributed around the globe. Some of the poorest and least-developed regions will be the ones required to adjust most rapidly to growing numbers. In most of the developed countries, there are likely to be only small increases or even decreases in total population size. For other countries, however, particularly in Africa, there will be a doubling or tripling in the number of people. Regions also differ in their levels of migration, both internal and international. These differences will in turn affect the degree of urbanization and the spatial distribution of people.

TABLE 1 Number of Countries by Population Density and Rate of Natural Increase (excluding city-states), 1991

Population Density (persons/sq. mi.)	Rate of Natural Increase (%)				Mean Rate of Natural Increase (%)
	0-1	1-2	2-3	3-4	
0-100	11	10	29	21	1.7
100-500	20	19	25	18	1.9
500-1,000	11	12	8	7	1.5
1,000-5,000	3	2	2	2	1.7

NOTE: The total number of countries is 200.

SOURCE: Data from Bureau of the Census (1991).

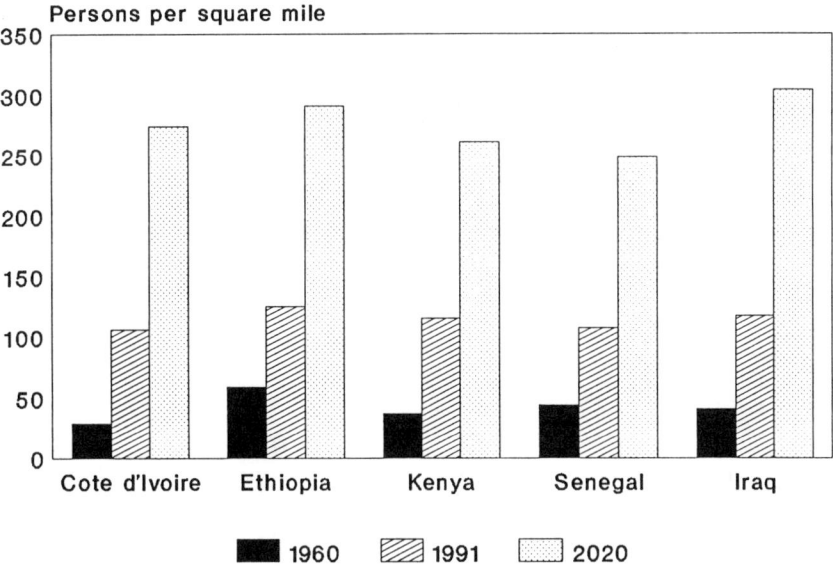

FIGURE 1 Countries whose 1991 population density is 100-150 percent of the world average and will at least double by the year 2020. SOURCE: Data from Bureau of the Census, international data base.

In studying the population and land use relationship, it is essential to consider both numbers of people and their behavior. Population growth influences land use patterns in combination with consumption behaviors and productive activities of the world's peoples. It is also essential to consider countries or regions in broader international context. Land use patterns in the developing world are sometimes strongly influenced by international trade and the high purchasing power of residents in the developed countries. The Committee on Population's Workshop on Population Growth and Land Use Change in Developing Countries was organized to look at some of these complex issues.

WORKSHOP PAPERS

Major points of both the workshop papers and discussions are summarized below. If a condensed paper is included in this volume, it is indicated.

M. Gordon Wolman's opening remarks, which are included in this volume, raise many of the questions that were pursued over the 2-day workshop. He stresses that people have always used and changed the way they

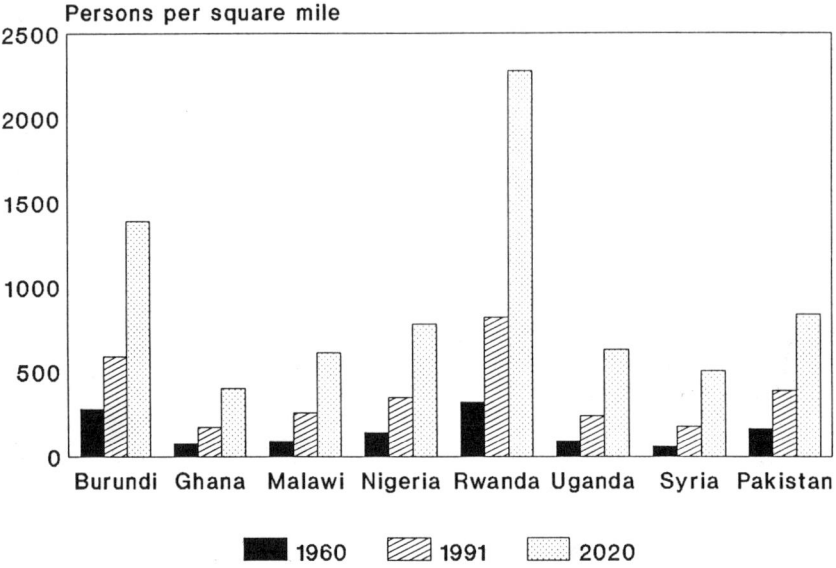

FIGURE 2 Countries whose 1991 population density is 150 percent or more of the world average and will at least double by the year 2020. SOURCE: Data from Bureau of the Census, international data base.

have used land from prehistoric time to the present. However, today's land use is qualitatively and quantitatively different from that in the past. Land use change has occurred at much faster rates as well as on much larger scales since 1900. It is difficult to evaluate these changes, partly due to the poor quality of available land use data and the difficulty of determining whether climate change or human activity has had the greatest effect on land use. Wolman questions whether the absolute size of the population or the rate of population increase has been more important in affecting land use change. He concludes that, given that the pace and types of land use change and population growth in the past are very different from those of today, the study of the past may not be the key to understanding the future.

In assessing the effects of changes in land use on the environment, Isaak S. Zonneveld's paper, which is included in this volume, discusses the importance of maintaining ecological integrity as land use changes. He describes the emergence of landscape ecology to study land form, function, and change. Zonneveld explains how and why land use change is measured and describes the strengths and weaknesses of remote sensing.

Steward Pickett's commentary, summarized in this volume, builds a bridge between the natural scientists' perspectives of Wolman and Zonneveld and the social science perspectives of the other papers. He discusses how ecologists tend to view the world from a micro perspective, whereas the social scientists tend to explain the world from a more macro perspective. Ecologists are shifting from studying ecosystems with little human intervention to analyzing the human dimensions of the ecological changes they document. He concludes by noting that "the battle to include humans in the scope of ecology is evidenced by the persistence of George Perkins Marsh's 'great question': 'Whether man is of nature or above her?'"

The discussions and papers by Hans Binswanger, Richard Bilsborrow and Martha Geores, and Uma Lele focus on the strengths and limitations of the neoclassical paradigm as stated by Ester Boserup (1965, 1970, 1981). Binswanger's discussion of his published research with Prabhu Pingali (1985) quantified how farmers responded to population growth through land intensification and extensification. Binswanger reviewed many of the innovations that farmers in developing countries make in the face of population pressures, such as irrigation, use of fertilizers, and multiple cropping. He also discussed the differences between the development of agriculture in the United States, which had relatively low population density, and in Japan, with high population density, to illustrate the different innovations farmers may make when faced with very different resource constraints.

Binswanger and Pingali's research concludes that, in growing populations, moderate increases in agricultural production are feasible with low-level land investments. However, a rapidly growing population will outstrip this agricultural production capacity without the intervention of science- and industry-based inputs, such as high-yielding seeds (Binswanger and Pingali, 1985).

Many factors can slow the speed of Boserupian responses. Uma Lele's paper and discussion outline the primary impediments operating in Africa. She notes that population is not distributed according to land quality because of high rates of vector-carried diseases in some areas and the placement of colonial infrastructure and European settlements. Macroeconomic policies that discriminate against agriculture distort market prices and thus people's responses to increased population size. The development of Western-style land tenure systems in Africa has sometimes led to the concentration of rights of access in certain groups and removed indigenous means of determining usage. In addition, poor credit markets and lack of technology suited for African agriculture have made the land intensification process more difficult.

Using cross-sectional data collected at the national level to quantify some of the relationships that Boserup's and Binswanger and Pingali's research identifies, Bilsborrow and Geores's paper finds a strong relationship between overall population density and the percentage of agricultural and pasture land used in production. Increases in fertilizer use have occurred widely across developing countries in recent decades as populations have grown, and this increased use has contributed to generalized increases in land productivity. However, the relationship between percentage changes in population and land used are not significant. Furthermore, the cross-sectional analysis among countries shows no relationship between density of population and the rate of depletion of forests. They document the poor quality of the data and the difficulty of doing cross-sectional analysis using data from developing countries. But they also suggest that this kind of research could be useful in identifying the key relationships to be pursued in more depth within countries.

Many of the conclusions of the Binswanger, Bilsborrow, and Lele presentations were illustrated in the case studies that were presented. (Four of these studies have been summarized and are included in this volume.) In fact, given the problems of making international comparisons and the limitations of current theories about how land use changes with increasing population density, the case studies of specific regions presented at the workshop became critical in better defining the issues and problems. Nigeria, India, Mauritius, Thailand, and Honduras were the countries discussed.

Rapid increases in population in northern Nigeria since the 1960s and the resultant land use changes are the subject of Michael Mortimore's paper, which is summarized in this volume. He demonstrates that the small-scale farmer invests considerably more in land improvement in the high-population-density area than in the low-density area to meet growing demands for food. In the high-density area, soil fertility is being managed on a sustainable basis. Given these results, he concludes that "population growth, and high population density, are compatible with sustainable resource management under smallholder conditions."

The effects of population growth and density on agricultural land use in India are examined in Robert Evenson's paper, which is included in this volume. He estimates the effects of population change on several agricultural investments during 1955-1987. The first stage of analysis shows that some of the investment in agricultural research, agricultural extension services, and rural infrastructure and net cropped area were induced by either population growth or increases in population density. However, many of these changes were also partly the result of strategic planning by the government. The second stage of analysis estimates the real returns to labor and to land by farmers as a function of population growth, technology flows, and infrastructure. Although population-induced changes in technology and infrastructure have a positive effect on real wage incomes, they are not sufficient to offset the negative effects of population growth.

The unique situation of Mauritius is studied by Wolfgang Lutz and Einar Holm in their paper, which is also summarized in this volume. Mauritius is an island country with high population density (and a low population growth rate) that has become increasingly integrated into world markets, making the effects of population change on land use highly indirect. Today, Mauritius imports much of its food and pays for it with its exports of textiles and sugar. As a result, since 1965, land previously used for sugar cane production has been progressively turned into urban space.

Theodore Panayotou's paper discusses Thailand's recent population growth and land use change. Between 1960 and 1990, the population doubled and the forested areas decreased 50 percent. He argues that the size of the agricultural population is the single most important determinant of the expansion of cultivated land. One of the contributing factors to land degradation in Thailand was that 40 percent of the agricultural land is held without land title, thereby reducing incentives for farmers to manage their land sustainably. Correlations suggested that deforestation in Thailand was related to the increase in population, the price of wood, and the poverty and low education level of the population.

The paper by Billie DeWalt, Susan Stonich, and Sarah Hamilton, included in this volume, evaluates the evidence linking population growth and the degradation of land and water resources in Honduras. They conclude that the deterioration of these resources is attributable more to unequal resource distribution and the patterns of commercial agricultural expansion than to population growth. They suggest that similar relationships exist in other Central American countries.

Vernon Ruttan's paper, included in this volume, returns to some of the issues raised by Wolman at the beginning of the workshop. He steps back from the focus of the case studies and discusses the implications of population growth and environmental change for agricultural production. He summarizes the historical concerns about sustainable growth. He then goes on to discuss institutional change and the problems of the differences in costs between private and social environmental services. He argues that scientific and technical constraints to increased agricultural production mean that agricultural research needs to be reorganized. "A serious effort to develop alternative land use, farming systems, and food systems scenarios for the 21st century should be initiated."

SUMMARY

Samuel Preston concluded the workshop by summarizing the general themes that were discussed and refined by the other participants on the effects of population growth on land use.

In the long run, population growth almost certainly affects land use patterns. The effects of population growth occur mainly through the extensification and intensification of agricultural production. Different population growth rates and different population densities probably produce different sets of land use changes. The evidence is partly logical. More people need more food, a situation that will affect how land is used for agriculture. The evidence is partly historical, as illustrated in M. Gordon Wolman's paper, which shows that land use patterns over the last 6,000 years are associated with the expansion of the human population. These associations have existed for over three decades in Thailand as documented in Theodore Panayotou's case study. There is also cross-sectional evidence, as illustrated in Richard Bilsborrow and Martha Geores's paper, that notes a correlation between a country's population density and the percentage of its arable land that is used in production. Finally, evidence based on Ester Boserup's model and research shows how population increases induce people to cultivate additional land or to farm their present land more productively, as demonstrated in Robert Evenson's paper.

Most of the changes in land use associated with very rapid population growth are likely to be disadvantageous for human beings. The changes that Boserup and others have described show that as populations grow, the technology required to maintain output is more expensive and requires more investment and labor. These are mainly the direct, on-site costs. There are also indirect, off-site costs that may be as great or greater than the on-site costs. They include salinization resulting from irrigation and contamination of common property resources (resources that are commonly owned, but without rules or regulations governing their use) from fertilizer use.

Many of the workshop participants thought the most important way to offset these costs associated with rapid population growth was through institutional change, such as property rights and agricultural research, as noted in Vernon Ruttan's paper. Whether these effects completely or partially offset the problems created by rapid population growth cannot be determined for the general case. But it is difficult to demonstrate an instance in which the offsetting effects are great enough to make the population as well off in terms of its land use patterns as it would have been with slower population growth. Evenson's paper shows that North India is not such an instance.

Population growth is not the only, or in many cases, the most important influence on land use. Other influences include technological change and changes in production techniques—which can be exogenous or, in some situations, endogenous or partly induced by population growth. National and international markets for goods and agricultural products clearly influence patterns of land use, as do government regulation and tax policies or the absence thereof. Income inequality was repeatedly mentioned by the workshop participants; clearly, it is an important factor in land use patterns in Honduras, as demonstrated in the Billie DeWalt, Susan Stonich, and Sarah Hamilton case study. Inequality itself, however, is in part influenced by rates of population growth.

In analyzing the question of whether population growth is the most important factor affecting land use, there are two issues—one is historical and one is prospective. What has been the relative influence of population growth on land use in the past? If the goal is to alter patterns of land use in the future, would reducing fertility be one of the most cost-effective ways to intervene?

Family planning programs put in place today will have their primary effect on the margin, which is the new births averted in the future. Looked at another way, however, population momentum simply means that if population policy is to have a major effect on future population growth patterns, it must begin sooner rather than later.

Because the effects of population growth on land use depend on many factors, case studies that clearly delineate the relative role of these factors are needed. Among these conditioning factors are markets for agricultural and forestry products, land tenure systems, soil quality, climate, and capital markets. The workshop case studies suggest that population growth is most likely to result in land degradation when land is held in common without rules governing its access, when production is mainly for subsistence, and when the soil is fragile and rainfall light. Under these conditions, fast population growth clearly creates potential for producing soil degradation. Parts of Africa may fit this pattern, but the northern Nigeria case study by Michael Mortimore shows that the farmers have adapted quite well to the doubling of their population.

With clear property rights, robust soils, and efficient markets, population growth is less likely to result in land degradation. Under these conditions, rapid population growth, which results in larger markets for agricultural products, gives land owners incentives to protect soil quality, which they are able to do by borrowing in relatively efficient capital markets. At the same time, land ownership provides collateral for the borrowing needed to invest in the protection of soil. Most real situations are somewhere between these two extreme scenarios, and more research is needed on the role of these conditioning factors in different areas.

Rapid population growth is likely to make the survival of other members of the animal and plant kingdom more difficult. Accompanying rapid population growth in the past has been greater species loss and a higher attrition within species than would have occurred in the absence of human expansion. It is difficult to place an exact value on this loss, particularly with regard to its importance for humans. There are widely varying views as to the weight that humans should attach to the welfare of other species. It is clear that the preferences for those species are not presently being reflected in any market mechanism, although the survival of several species is debated in the political process.

Better data are needed to analyze more definitively the relationship between population growth and land use. It was clear in the workshop discussion that many of the questions posed could not be answered with the available data. As Bilsborrow and Geores argued, additional time series data on land use variables are especially needed.

CONCLUSION

The research on resource limits has been less fruitful than research to determine the underlying dynamic relationships between population growth and land use change. Although many workshop participants recognized that all resources are not perfectly substitutable for one another, they agreed that conducting research on the effect of population growth on land use in terms of dynamics and interactions of factors was more useful than discussing the relationship in terms of fixed limits. Such an approach would mirror the continuing change in the many factors affecting land use and their interactions.

It was noted in conclusion that the workshop focused primarily on changes in the states or faces of the earth—how much deforestation is occurring, how much soil is being lost, etc. What needs more attention are changes in biogeochemical flows in which land use plays a major role. For example, feeding 10 billion people will require increased fertilizer use. If fertilization is intensified, methane production will increase, which may interfere with attempts to sustain the biosphere as we know it. Land use is an important factor, but it is related to many others that change with population growth.

Despite some careful research examining the relationship of population growth and land use change, we are still reviewing the beginning of an applied discipline rather than reviewing a mature body of research. The growing importance of these relationships to many countries is inconsistent with the lack of broad, systematic research attention. This lack of a thorough body of research, however, is due in part to some of the problems mentioned in this introduction. At this stage, methodological suggestions are easier to make than substantive conclusions.

Studies that rely on cross-sectional data cannot capture the dynamics between changes in population growth and land use change, as discussed by Bilsborrow and Geores. But historical time-series data rarely exist over the right time frame and scale to be useful. Pickett and Zonneveld illustrated the differences in scale that natural scientists and population experts use. Although correlations can be illustrative, causality is elusive. And, it is correlations and not documented casual relationships that have reinforced the work of the natural and social scientists in their different paradigms. Only carefully designed research to elucidate causality between population growth and land use change will help researchers address the fundamental differences in their paradigms.

The problems of scale and time horizon require that further research be focused on carefully designed and coordinated case studies, such as have been included in this volume. Indicators of how to measure and judge land use change need to be developed. Mortimore's case study of northern Nigeria suggests what some of the physical indicators might be; DeWalt's case study utilizes some of the social indicators. Only when there is a much larger number of sophisticated case studies will we be able to generalize about how current and future population growth rates in the world are likely to change land use.

This is the beginning of an important research area, not its culmination. Clearly the workshop papers and discussion raised more questions than they answered. The current population growth rates in some of the developing countries make this research not only important but essential to their ability to accommodate their future populations. Therefore, the questions raised by these workshop papers will be used to direct the subsequent work of the Committee on Population and, we hope, others in this area with the purpose of stimulating new research on the relationship between population growth and land use change in the future.

REFERENCES

Binswanger, H.P., and P.L. Pingali
    1985   Population growth and technological change in agriculture. Pp. 62-89 in T.J. Davis, ed., *Proceedings of the Fifth Agriculture Sector Symposium: Population and Food*. Washington, D.C.: World Bank.

Boserup, E.
    1965   *The Conditions of Agricultural Growth: The Economics of Agrarian Change Under Population Pressure*. Chicago: Aldine Press.
    1970   Present and potential food production in developing countries. Pp. 100-113 in W. Zelinsky et al., eds., *Geography and a Crowding World*. New York: Oxford University Press.
    1981   *Population and Technological Change*. Chicago: University of Chicago Press.

Brown, L.R., A. Durning, C. Flavin, H. French, J. Jacobson, N. Lenssen, M. Lowe, S. Postel, M. Renner, J. Ryan, L. Starke, and J. Young
    1991   *State of the World 1991: A Worldwatch Institute Report on Progress Toward a Sustainable Society*. New York: W.W. Norton.

Bureau of the Census
    1991   *World Population Profile: 1991*. Report WP/91. Washington, D.C.: U.S. Department of Commerce.

Ehrlich, P.R., and J.P. Holdren
    1971   Impact of population growth. *Science* 171:1212-1217.

Ehrlich, P.R., A.H. Ehrlich, and J.P. Holdren
    1977   *Ecoscience: Population, Resources, Environment*. San Francisco: Freeman.

Higgins, G.M., A.H. Kassam, L. Naiken, G. Fischer, and M.M. Shah
    1983   *Potential Population Supporting Capacities of Lands in the Developing World*. Rome: Food and Agriculture Organization.

Lele, U., and S. Stone
    1989   *Population Pressure, the Environment and Agricultural Intensification: Variations on the Boserup Hypothesis.* Madia Discussion Paper 4. Washington, D.C.: World Bank.

Malthus, T.R.
    1798   An essay on the principle of population. Reprinted, pp. 15-139 in P. Appleman, ed., *An Essay on the Principle of Population.* New York: W.W. Norton., 1976.

Raven, P.H.
    1991   Winners and losers in the twentieth-century struggle to survive. Pp. 259-266 in K. Davis and M.S. Bernstam, eds., *Resources, Environment, and Population: Present Knowledge and Future Options.* A supplement to Vol. 16, 1990, *Population and Development Review.* New York: The Population Council and Oxford University Press.

Schmink, M., and C.H. Wood
    1987   The political ecology of Amazonia. Pp. 38-57 in P.D. Little and M.M. Horowitz, eds., *Lands at Risk in the Third World: Local Level Perspectives.* Boulder, Colo.: Westview Press.

Simon, J.
    1981   *The Ultimate Resource.* Princeton, N.J.: Princeton University Press.

Stiglitz, J.E.
    1979   Neoclassical analysis of resource economics. Pp. 36-66 in K. Smith, ed., *Scarcity and Growth Reconsidered.* Baltimore, Md.: The Johns Hopkins University Press.

United Nations, Department of International Economic and Social Affairs
    1991   *World Population Prospects 1990.* No. 120. New York: United Nations.

World Bank
    1992   *World Development Report 1992: Development and the Environment.* New York: Oxford University Press.

2

Population, Land Use, and Environment: A Long History

M. Gordon Wolman

We can surmise that human beings have been altering the environment throughout the several million years they have inhabited the earth. Artifacts testify to the distribution and intensity of these alterations. Moreover, some reconstructions of human population numbers over time suggest step-like increases in the number of people on the globe with the advent of successive major technological revolutions including the domestication of animals, the advent of agriculture, and the Industrial Revolution. Brief vignettes of the distribution of human activities at selected moments in history coupled with estimates of the kinds of impacts these activities apparently made on the environment provide a perspective on the modern scene. Despite large changes in land and environment in the past, the evidence suggests that the modern global combination of a very large population base, relatively rapid rates of population growth, and very rapid rates of technological change constitute a unique assemblage in human history, an assemblage posing new hurdles to adaptation and enhancing the rate of change.

NATURAL PROCESSES AND ANTHROPOGENIC IMPACTS

Because the earth is a dynamic system, changes to the land, water, and air caused by human activities must be seen in this dynamic context. Not only are there cycles of land formation and denudation, oscillations of continents and oceans, and movements of water and air at scales ranging from

TABLE 1 Climate and Related Conditions at Selected Times in the Past

Approximate Date	Climate and Related Conditions
10,000 BP	End of glaciation, glacier retreat, rapid rise of sea level, wet period North Africa and equatorial lakes
8,000 - 7,000 BP	Hypsithermal — warmer, drier Sahara
6,000 BP	Rate of sea level rise slowing, Strait of Dover open
5,000 BP	Brief cold period, Stone Age
4,500 BP	Increasing aridity in drylands, warmest post-glacial period
1 AD	Continuing warm in Europe
800 - 1000 AD	Warmer, Norse in Greenland, medieval warm period
1500 AD	Little Ice Age (1300 - 1700 AD) Europe
1800 AD	Temperature somewhat lower than present
Present	Warmer than late 19th century

NOTE: BP: before the present.

SOURCE: Data from Lamb (1982) and Jäger and Barry (1990).

seconds to millennia, but also slow or punctuated evolutionary changes in biota are a continuing phenomenon. Similarly, climate as well as landscape and vegetation has fluctuated greatly during the brief interval of human occupance of the earth (Table 1). Thus the impact of population numbers or of population and technological change cannot be evaluated in the absence of some knowledge of the behavior of the "natural" scene. Understanding the vicissitudes of the natural system is particularly important in evaluating efforts at remediation of human impacts and in assessing the degree to which particular impacts are likely to be manageable if not reversible within varying periods of time. Temporal and spatial scales, however, are interrelated. For example, as small parcels of land are changed within a forest, upon abandonment the surrounding forest may readily provide seed for regeneration. In contrast, extensive cutting of forests for agriculture may leave only small refuges of original plants and animals, reducing the likelihood of regeneration of some of the biota and increasing the duration of transformation. Human beings have altered the land at varying rates and over vastly different areas. Many of these changes can be seen in the historical record.

HISTORICAL CHANGES IN HUMAN ACTIVITIES ON THE LAND

A selection from a series of maps of land use provided by Simmons (1987) provides a base for a rapid review of the nature of the changes in the land created by human activities (Figure 1). Ten thousand years before the present (BP), shortly after rapid retreat of recent continental glaciers began, agriculture was practiced on only a tiny portion of the land. Hunting and gathering remained the principal sources of food. By 6,000 years BP, agriculture existed in the Middle East and across the continent of Europe and in South Asia. Agriculture included upland farming, irrigation in the broad bottomlands of the major river valleys such as the Nile and the Indus and the practice of floodwater farming in small valleys on semiarid hillslopes. The impact of agriculture on the upland, including deforestation and grazing, particularly on limestone terrain, has long been recognized. In Palestine, Greece, Turkey, and North Africa, soil was eroded to bedrock in many places and nearby harbors sedimented with silt (Marsh, 1864). The former harbor of Ephesus in Turkey, for example, extended well inland from the present shoreline of the Aegean Sea, the result of both human activity and climatic variability. In Palestine, the Judean hills were deforested in Roman time and to some extent before. Degradation of the uplands resulted in the development of swamps in coastal and freshwater areas. Although the goat is often blamed for grazing the land down to bare rock, many practices led to erosion in semiarid regions. In places, however, bare rock is attributable to the weathering of limestone containing no residuals from which to constitute a soil after solution of the limestone. Contrary to the view of some, the evidence indicates that "the land of milk and honey" in the desert was at best an exaggeration. Although it has been argued that the evidence of floodwater farming, extensive terracing on the uplands, and the existence of many archaeological sites in areas of the Middle East, particularly Palestine, indicate the existence of large populations, careful dating of remains suggests that populations fluctuated over periods of hundreds of years. Not all sites were occupied simultaneously (Evenari et al., 1971). Many, particularly near the Mediterranean, were related to trade routes, and it cannot be presumed that larger settlements were supported solely by local produce and pasture.

In contrast, large-scale irrigation development in the Middle East and in Asia was associated with larger populations and with greater impacts on the resource itself. In Mesopotamia, irrigation development was associated with urbanization (Adams, 1981). Early stratigraphic and archaeological records found in the Tigris basin also reveal successive periods of successful irrigation interrupted by siltation of canals and salinization of the soil, problems resulting from inadequate application of water and poor mainte-

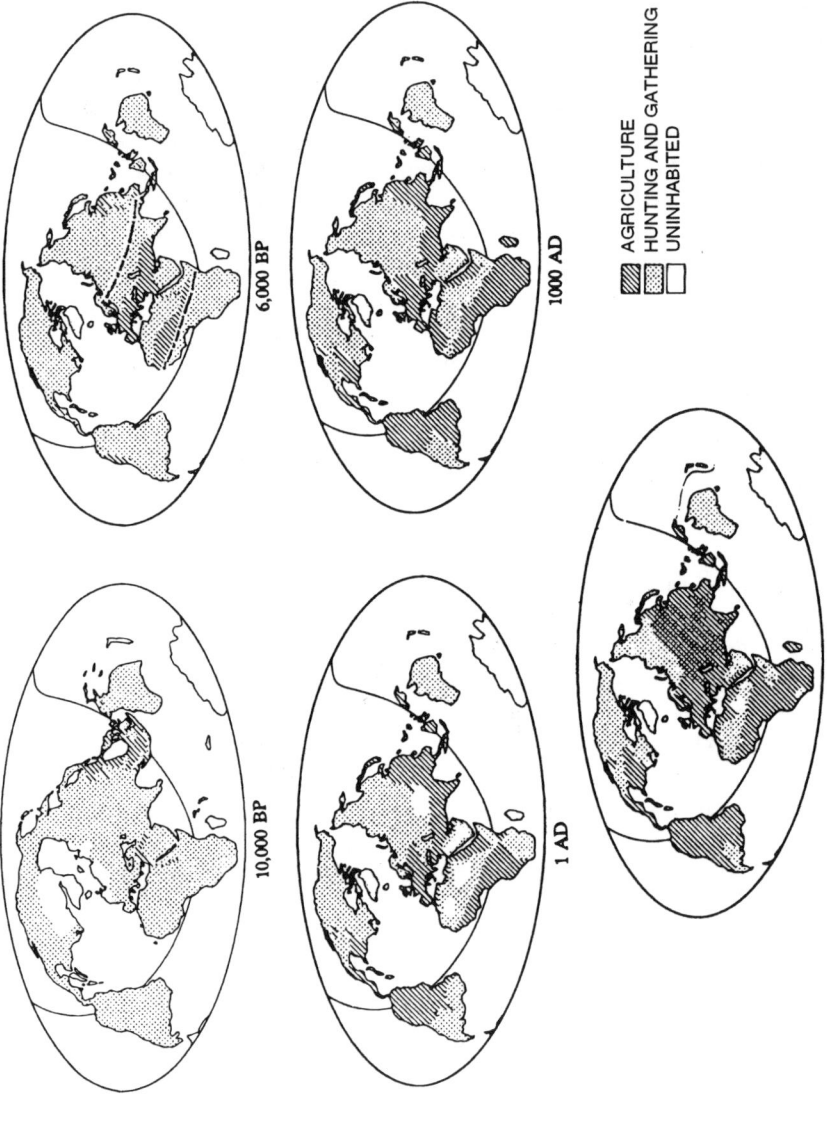

FIGURE 1 Spread of human modification of the earth. (See Table 1 for prevailing climatic conditions.) SOURCE: Maps from Simmons (1987).

nance. Precisely these same problems are encountered in modern irrigated agriculture (Shanan, 1992; Whitcombe, 1972).

In the Indus valley, extensive irrigation development at Harrapa involved changes in land use, including an extensive urban center. Alternative explanations, including climatic change and mismanagement of the irrigation base, have been credited with causing the demise of this civilization (Lamb, 1982). Again, in the modern era in this region, huge irrigation developments in the nineteenth-century colonial period in India not only produced large increases in production but also, over time, were plagued with predicted problems of salinization and waterlogging. These huge irrigation systems were carefully designed and continue to operate today, although in a number of areas careful management is required to provide water while also improving drainage by lowering high water tables. Population has grown significantly, and irrigation and new crop varieties have contributed to large increases in food production (Buringh and Dudal, 1987).

The Nile valley reflects a similar alteration of the landscape over a period of thousands of years. Agriculture was initially practiced in natural riverine wetlands to the south. Over time natural systems were altered, and several thousand years ago embankments constructed on the floodplain held water in place after flooding, permitting extensive basin irrigation (Butzer, 1976). Over the centuries, salinization has not been a problem.

Large-scale irrigation in the past, and at present, transforms the landscape. Degradation by salinization and waterlogging may accompany such changes, but these effects have often been avoided or reversed with proper maintenance and operation. Little evidence suggests that the benefits of increased production associated with irrigation were historically either overwhelmed by increases in population or by deterioration of the environment. At the same time, irrigated lands have been abandoned or allowed to deteriorate as a result of a variety of factors, including war and social upheavals, devastating floods, and perhaps changes in climate (Whitney, 1984).

By 1500 agriculture had spread throughout much of the world, including Asia, Latin America, Africa, and North America (Figure 1). Brief consideration of a few localities and different farming techniques is instructive. In Europe, the landscape was completely transformed between 900 and 1900 AD (Figure 2), as forest clearing and land drainage created pastures and agricultural fields. Over time, different styles of farming characterized portions of the landscape. Stumps were left in places to regenerate trees for firewood. Hedges were planted to mark fields and contain livestock. In the present era these hedges are being removed to enlarge fields to ease mechanical tillage. In Europe and New England, soils have been improved by drainage and by application of fertilizers transforming them to their present productive agricultural condition (U.S. Department of Agriculture, 1954). Illustrative are the enormous changes that have taken place since

FIGURE 2 Change in forest cover from 900 AD to 1900 AD in Europe (cited in Darby, 1956).

European settlement in eastern North America. Originally nearly entirely forested, by the late nineteenth century virtually 80 percent of the New England landscape was in agriculture. A nearly complete reversal has occurred in the subsequent 100 years. Much of New England is again heavily forested, and in some areas forests again cover nearly 80 percent of the land (Raup and Carlson, 1941).

The transformation of the European agricultural landscape has been accompanied by increases in agricultural productivity. Whereas productivity remained relatively constant for the prior several hundred years, crop yields began to increase in the seventeenth century and, in the nineteenth century, wheat yields in England, for example, increased by about 50 percent. Truly revolutionary increases in productivity have occurred in the last 50 years with the introduction of new plant varieties and large-scale application of fertilizers, herbicides, and pesticides (Grigg, 1980). Earlier increases in productivity were a product of the reduction of fallow, increases in labor input, and the application of manure. These significant transformations in the land have supported increasingly dense populations. Intensive modern agriculture including the application of large quantities of nutrients, particularly nitrogen, as well as synthetic organic compounds, poses new problems of land and groundwater contamination (Ministry of Agriculture, Fisheries and Food, 1976).

Because padi rice production, established before 1500 AD (Figure 1), represents one of the most significant changes on the landscape in Asia, comment is warranted on the impact of such changes. The padi system includes the application of nitrogen with the use of blue-green algae (in some ways analogous to the use of legumes in Europe) and maintenance of constant water levels, particularly in coastal deltas where nutrients are delivered in suspension and solution. Heavy clay soils allow a minimum of seepage losses of water and nutrients and, as the land is covered with water, it is not exposed to high temperature. Historically, small increases in productivity have been primarily associated with progressive increases in labor input. Patterns were apparently established in Asia and Southeast Asia in the eleventh and twelveth centuries with high rural densities in Southern China, Korea, Japan, much of Java, and parts of the Phillipines. Continuous padi agriculture is perhaps one of the best examples of continuous management of a sustainable resource. Major increases in rice productivity have occurred in the last 50 years in Japan with the application of fertilizer, new varieties, and new technology.

A very different but widespread agriculture practice, shifting cultivation or bush fallowing, has altered the landscape for centuries (Pelzer, 1945). Forest trees are felled, and stumps and trunks burned both to clear the land and to provide some fertilizer. Crops, including cereals and wheats or yams and cassava, are planted in the clearing. Forests provide shade over small plots, and no weeding is done. As weeds become prevalent and crop yields decline, new land is cleared for cultivation.

The cropping cycle in many areas is on the order of 3 to 5 years. Where population densities are low, the return cycle of cultivation might be as long as 25 years. As population densities increase, the fallow cycle shortens and grasses as well as legumes may be planted. Occasionally, but rarely, livestock may be grazed on the fallow plot.

Increasing population has been associated with shortening of the fallow period and limitation of the regenerative time provided for forest growth and restoration of the soil. Without the application of fertilizer and careful tillage and management practices, progressive reduction of the fallow period will reduce the productive capacity of the land (Grigg, 1987). Where larger areas are cleared in tropical forests underlain by heavily weathered soils, Lal (1985) and others have shown that removal of vegetation may lead not only to rapid erosion but also to degradation of the structure of the soil, as erosion by rainfall and runoff alternates with drying of the surface. A hardpan may develop that can greatly reduce the productivity of the land. Land degradation, then, is a function of clearing, the duration of fallow, and the mode of agriculture including the choice of crops. In some tropical regions, recovery of the productivity of the land may be difficult if not impossible as a result of the loss of soil, reduction of tilth, and removal of nutrients. It can be argued that the loss of productivity of the land resulting from reduction of fallow periods is directly attributable to increasing rates of population growth outstripping the land available for rotations of clearing. Reduced fallow in the absence of fertilizer or nutrient replacement does reduce potential productivity. A number of papers elsewhere in this volume debate the cause and effect relationship between population growth and land deterioration.

In the eighteenth and nineteenth centuries, the major grain regions of eastern Europe, North America, and Australia had come under development. Continuous row cropping and monoculture in these regions has led some to suggest that the land has been seriously degraded (see Larson et al., 1983). The evidence is equivocal. In the United States, as the population spread west, agricultural production increased. Conversion of grassland to agriculture, it is estimated, increased erosion of the land surface on average roughly two times the natural background (Schumm and Harvey, 1982). Such estimates must be based on the accumulation of sediments in stream valleys and not on the land itself. At the same time, climatic variations during the Holocene period have resulted in alternating periods of erosion and deposition in stream valleys (Ruhe and Daniels, 1965). Although the estimates of erosion suggest that the overall rate of erosion increased during the intensification of agriculture, there is no evidence from records of sediment transport in the lower Mississippi River that the materials eroded from the land have reached the lower portion of the river. Much sediment may well be stored throughout the river system below the fields and in the upstream portions of many of the major rivers. Storage of such material is well documented in valleys and in reservoirs throughout the Middle West and Great Plains of the United States. Large reservoirs, such as the succession of major dams and impoundments on the Missouri River, now store large quantities of sediment. Unlike the potential impact of land erosion, the impact of storage of sediment in reservoirs is seen by roughly a one-third reduction in the amount of sediment transported in the lower Mississippi River (Williams and Wolman, 1984). On the land itself, inorganic fertilizers have compensated for natural losses in natural organic material, increasing productivity and masking losses of the original material. Much debate continues over the potential impact of machinery and modern technology on the long-term structure and character of the soils in these productive regions. Similarly, although erosion has removed the upper portions of the soil in places, in the Midwest where soil horizons are deep, the impact on productivity in agriculture has been limited (Larson et al., 1983).

For the Ukraine, one of the most productive grain lands in the world, it has been suggested that continuous row-cropping has resulted in a loss of organic matter and structure and in soil fertility. Little field evidence, however, appears to support such claims (Wolman, 1985). To the extent that degradation is taking place, one may speculate that adequate management might restore fertility and structure, although yields suggest that such management has not been practiced in many areas during the last 70 years.

OFF-SITE EFFECTS OF LAND CHANGES

It is important to note, particularly in the context of the modern scene, that changes on the land cascade to the hydrologic system in rivers, lakes,

TABLE 2 Relationship of Wet and Dry Periods: Nanticoke River, Chesapeake Bay

Time Period	Sedimentation: Rate cm yr^{-1}	Charcoal: M^2 cm^{-2} yr^{-1}	Pollen Ratio: Dry to Wet
European			
1700-1980	0.17	6.8	2.9
Little Ice Age			
1300-1700	0.05	2.2	2.4
Middle Warm			
800-1300	0.15	15.5	4.1
Early			
600-800	0.07	9.7	3.4

NOTE: Changes reflect the off-site effects of changes on the landscape, including the significant impact of land clearance for agriculture by Europeans.

SOURCE: Data from G. Brush, Johns Hopkins University.

estuaries, and the coastal ocean. As L'vovich and White (1990) have shown, human activities have significantly altered the global distribution of runoff in rivers. They estimate an increase over a period of 300 years of about 20 percent in base flow and a decrease of 16 percent in surface runoff as a result of anthropogenic activities, including deforestation for agriculture, drainage, and reservoir construction. More dramatic is a 300 percent increase in consumptive use of water in irrigated agriculture over the last 300 years. For the globe as a whole, aggregate consumptive water uses represent a modest percentage of total runoff, but the magnitudes represent large fractions of available runoff in regions such as the Colorado, Nile, and Indus basins.

At a very different scale, work by Brush (1992, personal communication) in the Chesapeake Bay region shows the close relationship between changes in land use, climatic variations, and the impact on water bodies. Some conclusions are suggested by the data in Table 2, which shows the sequence of changes in sedimentation rate, charcoal content, and ratios of pollen representing vegetation favoring dry and wetter environments. First, the bay tributaries experienced different rates of deposition of sediment, charcoal, and pollen during dry and wet periods. Second, the profile of pollen ratios indicates alternating periods of dry and wet conditions. Third, the period of European settlement from 1700 to 1980 is characterized by very high sedimentation rates, although similar sedimentation rates are also associated with earlier periods from 800 to 1300 AD, a warm period in the climatic record prior to western settlement. This warm period is also associated with a high rate of charcoal deposition. The combination of dryness, indicated by the pollen composition and charcoal, as well as the rapid sedimentation rate suggests that natural forest fires may have occurred periodically, exposing the soil to rapid rates of erosion with sediment and charcoal transported to the depositional site in the tributary. Thus, marked natural variations as well as anthropogenic effects are seen in the record. Associations of landscape change and changes in water quality are of major importance. Currently these are referred to as on-site and off-site impacts or damages, and they are the same as those noted earlier in the Middle East. The difference lies in the extent and scale of operation on the landscape in those parts of the world where conservation farming is limited.

SOME GENERALIZATIONS FROM THE PAST

A few simple but important conclusions may be drawn from this brief review of past changes in landscape associated with human activities. First, human beings have altered much of the world's land. The most significant changes have been those associated with all kinds of agriculture. The capacity to alter the landscape has increased with technology, and land use change in many areas has accelerated (Buringh and Dudal, 1987). Roughly one-half of what might be referred to as the "usable" rural land has now been modified in one way or another. Until recently most of the increase in agricultural production has been through the expansion of land, shortening of fallow, and the increase in labor. Most of the accelerated increase in agricultural productivity in the past half century is associated with the application of fertilizers and new plant varieties. Increase in the use of herbicides and insecticides made of new synthetic organic compounds unknown in nature poses potential environmental problems not significant in the earlier historical record.

Although major transformations of the landscape in the historical record are clearly recognizable, it is much more difficult to determine the kinds, and particularly the magnitudes, of changes to the land and water associated with changes in land use. It is even more difficult to relate these to population. Transformation of European and American forest lands to agriculture, for example, is seen by some as deterioration of the environment. In contrast, most agriculturists see such changes as improvement, making wetsoils and wetlands tillable and productive. Valuing or balancing gains and losses then resulting from historical land changes is exceedingly difficult. Terraces, irrigation, forest clearance, drainage and cropping are improvements under many circumstances. Yet they also alter the environment, and some may be irreversible. Even irreversibility, however, may not be prima facie evidence of negative value, although cumulative degradation of a finite resource for which no real substitute exists poses a significant problem of value.

A very different problem arises in distinguishing between human and natural impacts on the landscape. Climate in most of the world has fluctuated throughout much of the Holocene period. These fluctuations, well recorded in the stratigraphic record, are reflected in significant changes on the landscape in the absence of human intervention. Overgrazing or cropping may complicate the record, and make discerning the relative importance of human versus natural processes more difficult. In addition, while the archaeological record may reflect movements of population into and out of a region, the causes of migrations often remain unknown.

Distinguishing between the influence of human beings on the landscape and natural processes has become increasingly difficult as a result of recent recognition of the dynamism of landscape evolution. Earlier concepts of landscape equilibrium implied that vegetation, soil, and erosional processes achieved a relatively stable configuration under a particular prevailing climate. Additional work has demonstrated that such equilibria, if they exist, are exceedingly dynamic. Particular emphasis is placed upon the importance of disturbance of the landscape by episodic events of large magnitude such as hurricanes, fires, and floods. Each major event may result in a new potentially stable assemblage of vegetation. The sequence of changes following disturbance and the duration of an apparently stable configuration are difficult to predict. As these disturbances interact with human activities, isolation of the significance of one or the other influence is particularly difficult.

Another important element in evaluating the significance of the impact of human activities on the landscape involves the concept of recovery and resilience. Resilience refers to the ability of the landscape or ecological system to rebound from the impacts of instant or progressive change. Recovery refers to the process by which an absolute change, whether achieved rapidly or slowly, can be mitigated or reversed to return a system to its prior undisturbed state. Unfortunately, little information is available about recovery processes or about the extent to which initial conditions in the environment and in the land itself have been altered over long periods of time. Dramatic examples of erosion and soil losses where farming is practiced on very steep slopes without terracing are important and easily documented (Eckholm, 1976). They cannot be extrapolated to different settings. It is much more difficult to recognize slower or more subtle changes over time or to evaluate the likelihood that such changes can be reversed. Dregne (1991), an astute soil scientist with worldwide experience, estimates that about 70 percent of "global drylands" are degraded, with rangelands suffering the most extensive degradation. He notes, however, that, "data on land degradation are so difficult to obtain that a study in 100 countries is largely based on a few maps, a little experimental data, observation and even anecdotes" (Dregne, 1991:20-21).

Until recently, relatively little interest was expressed in the off-site effects of changes on the landscape. While sedimentation of waterways was important historically, current interest concerns organic and inorganic substances attached to sediment particles. Metals, petroleum products, pesticides, herbicides, and all of the materials used in modern industrial societies can be found in the accumulated sediments.

A broad survey of landscape change effected by human beings throughout human history clearly demonstrates that human beings have significantly altered the natural landscape over much of the globe. In many instances such change has degraded soil and water. Elsewhere the "made" landscape has been made more productive, if not more diverse. Much less clear is the degree to which degradation of these resources is reversible in whole or in part. (Whether this is a desirable objective is a separate question). Even less clear is the degree to which population numbers or rates of change have been directly or indirectly the driving force behind degradative or restorative processes.

THE PAST AND THE FUTURE

Most of the experience of the past summarized here cannot be extrapolated into the future. To the extent that the dryland degradation reported by Dregne (1991) is recent and expanding, more of the same suggests further losses. Similar statements apply to exploitation of steep lands and areas denuded of vegetation and exposed to intense rainfall. Projections, paraphrasing Dubos, are not predictions. Although degradative trends are probably reversible in many regions, it is worth noting that soil conservation practice in Africa and in many parts of Latin America and Asia has probably been retreating rather than advancing in the last several decades. Social and economic factors rather than knowledge or technology appear to determine this trend (Blaikie, 1985). Under some circumstances "conservation pays," but much evidence demonstrates that conservation often "costs" someone, whether an individual farmer or a government.

While they do not discuss degradation or deterioration in the land resource, Buringh and Dudal (1987) projected changes or losses in land uses between 1975 and 2000. They note expected declines in some highly productive agricultural lands due to urban expansion, but agricultural expansion is expected to occur at the expense of forests and grazing land. Whether such conversions are viewed as positive or negative, contributions to society and the environment depends on the long-term values placed on these resources.

Limited documentation of the relation between population change and land change lends caution to extrapolation into the future of observations of yield declines where sedentary agriculture replaces shifting cultivation, where salinization and waterlogging accompany modern irrigation systems, or where agriculture replaces forests as population grows. At the same time, the resilience or adaptability of the land surface to the ends of human beings in the past may not be a proper measure of the prospects for the future.

The modern scene is not like the past. Both the rate and the magnitude of population change are large, the magnitude unprecedented in history. Although fertility is declining in many parts of the world, the increase in world population of about 1 billion people in the last decade is equal to the total world population in 1800 (Raven et al., 1993). Previous population expansions have neither been as large nor have they occurred on a comparable unexpandable base. Of course, earlier generations may have perceived themselves in similar predicaments. A second factor is again one of rate and magnitude. The rate of production of new and particularly synthetic materials unknown in nature places additional burdens on the environment. These materials may accumulate, degrade, or move from place to place, altering the quality of the landscape in new ways. Third, the off-site impacts of changes on the land are recognized as increasingly important. Today the human capacity to alter the environment is on a scale equivalent to the forces of nature, a condition that did not prevail in the past (Wolman, 1990).

The absence of satisfactory historical information relating both land and population change to the many factors that influence both suggests the obvious need for comparative studies combining demography, land use, and environmental change. Measurement of land or environmental change is difficult. Moreover, quantitative and comparable measurements are needed over time, but these must be both diagnostic and yet sufficiently simple that they can be extended to a wide range of conditions. Modern technology including observations from space and the use of geographic information systems is gradually making it possible to observe changes over large areas on reasonable time scales. These spatial observations, however, must be combined with observations on the ground not only to correlate observed changes with spectral images, but also to determine the quantitative effects of various uses of the land on the land and environment.

Information about the spatial distribution of populations is essential. The impact of population growth on the land will be influenced by the distribution among rural village or urban metropolitan areas. Environmental effects have different spatial characteristics at local, regional (drainage basin), national, continental, and global scales. Measures of population must be correlative with the presumed scale of impacts.

The tenor of the present debate over projections of land change, population, and environmental degradation appears more pessimistic today than were the global food production models projected a few years ago. It is not clear whether this is due to increasing evidence of deterioration or to pessimism with respect to remedial or corrective measures. The factors affecting demographic change are enormously complex. No doubt many institutions and conditions affect the outcome including land tenure, poverty, conversion to cash crops, the performance of the market, and transportation. The way in which these elements interact with or influence the environment is, of course, inseparable from this complexity. It should be possible to evaluate more precisely the effect of people on the land and on the environment in different settings. The case examples that follow in this volume both illustrate and explicate some of this complexity.

REFERENCES

Adams, R. McC.
    1981   *Heartland of Cities*. Chicago: University of Chicago Press.

Blaikie, P.
    1985   *The Political Economy of Soil Erosion in Developing Countries*. New York: Longman.

Buringh, P., and R. Dudal
    1987   Patterns of land use in space and time. In M.G. Wolman and F.G.A. Fournier, eds., *Land Transformation in Agriculture*. New York: Wiley (SCOPE).

Butzer, K.W.
    1976   *Early Hydraulic Civilization in Egypt: A Study in Cultural Ecology*. Chicago: University of Chicago Press.

Darby, H.C.
    1956   The clearing of the woodland in Europe. Pp. 183-216 in W.L. Thomas, Jr., ed., *Man's Role in Changing the Face of the Earth*. Chicago: University of Chicago Press.

Dregne, H.E.
    1991   Arid land degradation: a result of mismanagement. *Geotimes* 36:19-21.

Eckholm, E.P.
    1976   *Losing Ground*. New York: W.W. Norton.

Evenari, M., L. Shanan, and N. Tadmor
    1971   *The Negev: Challenge of a Desert*. Cambridge, Mass.: Harvard University Press.

Grigg, D.
    1980   *Population Growth and Agrarian Change: An Historical Perspective*. Cambridge Geographical Studies. Cambridge, Eng.: Cambridge University Press.
    1987   The industrial revolution and land transformation. In M.G. Wolman and F.G.A. Fournier, eds., *Land Transformation in Agriculture*. New York: Wiley (SCOPE).

Jäger, J., and R.G. Barry
    1990   Climate. Pp. 335-351 in B.L. Turner et al., eds., *The Earth as Transformed by Human Action*. Cambridge, England: Cambridge University Press.

Lal, R.
    1985   Soil erosion and its relation to productivity in tropical soils. Pp. 237-247 in S.A. El-swaify, W.C. Moldenhauer, and A. Lo, eds., *Soil Erosion and Conservation*. Ibadan, Nigeria: International Institute of Tropical Agriculture.

Lamb, H.H.
    1982   *Climate History and the Modern World*. London: Methuen.

Larson, W.E., F.J. Pierce, and R.H. Dowdy
    1983   The threat of soil erosion to long-term crop production. *Science* 219:458-465.

L'vovich, M.I., and G.F. White
    1990   Use and transformation of terrestrial water systems. In B.L. Turner et al., eds.,

The Earth as Transformed by Human Action. Cambridge, England: Cambridge University Press.

Marsh, G.P
 1864 *Man and Nature or Physical Geography as Modified by Human Action.* London: Sampson Low.

Ministry of Agriculture, Fisheries and Food
 1976 *Agriculture and Water Quality.* Her Majesty's Stationery Office.

Pelzer, K.J
 1945 Pioneer Settlements in the Asiatic Tropics. Special publication no. 25, *American Geographic Society*, New York.

Raup, H.M., and R.E. Carlson
 1941 *The History of Land Use in the Harvard Forest.* Harvard Forest Bulletin no. 20, Petersham, Mass.

Raven, P.H., L.R. Berg, and G.B. Johnson
 1993 *Environment.* Forth Worth, Tx.: Saunders.

Ruhe, R.V., and R.B. Daniels
 1965 Landscape erosion—geologic and historic. *Journal of Soil Water Conservation.* 20:52-57.

Schumm, S.A., and M.D. Harvey
 1982 Natural erosion in the U.S.A. Pp. 15-22 in B.L. Schmidt et al., eds., *Determinants of Soil Loss Tolerance.* Special Publication 45. American Society of Agronomy and Soil Science Society of America, Madison, Wis.

Shanan, L.
 1992 Planning and management of irrigation systems in developing countries. *Agricultural Water Management* 22(1-2):1-234.

Simmons, I.G.
 1987 Transformation of the land in pre-industrial time. Pp. 45-75 in M.G. Wolman and F.G.A. Fournier, eds., *Land Transformation in Agriculture.* New York: Wiley (SCOPE).

U.S. Department of Agriculture
 1954 *The Changing Fertility of New England Soils.* Agriculture Information Bulletin No. 1333. Washington D.C.: U.S. Department of Agriculture.

Whitcombe, E.
 1972 *Agrarian Conditions in Northern India,* Vol. I. The United Provinces under British Rule. Berkeley: University of California Press.

Whitney, J.W.
 1984 The Geology and Geomorphology of the Helmand Basin Afghanistan: A Study of the Environmental and Geologic Processes that Affected the Survival of Desert Civilizations in Sistan. Ph.D. dissertation, University of Michigan microfilm.

Williams, G.P., and M.G. Wolman
 1984 *Downstream Effects of Dams on Alluvial Rivers.* U.S. Geological Survey Professional Paper 1286. Washington, D.C.

Wolman, M.G.
 1985 Soil erosion and crop productivity: A worldwide prospective. Pp. 9-21 in R.F. Follett and B.A. Stewart, eds., *Soil Erosion and Crop Productivity.* Madison, Wis.: ASA-CSSA-SSSA.

Wolman, M.G.
 1990 The impact of man. *EOS* 71:1884-1886.

3

What Is Meant by Land Use Change?

Isaak S. Zonneveld

LANDSCAPE STABILITY

Because of the vertical and horizontal heterogeneity of landscapes, researchers from many disciplines use land survey data. Zoologically oriented landscape ecologists study the effects of horizontal heterogeneity on animal populations (Merriam, 1984; Forman, 1982). Similarly, the data can be used to help answer a key question for humankind: Is the survival of groups of people essentially dependent on landscape heterogeneity? Agriculture and other human activities imply it is.

Landscape ecology is concerned with the study of land or landscape, its form, function, and genesis (change). It looks at the factors interacting at the earth's surface, including the physical, biological, and noospherical actions originated by humans. These factors form three-dimensional phenomena that can be seen as horizontal patterns of related elements (units of land) and as vertical patterns of land attributes, such as climate, rock, soil, water, and vegetation. The heterogeneity of these patterns is the main focus of landscape ecology.

A landscape is viewed as a holistic entity that is composed of a variety of relationships in a relatively steady state. The maintenance of a steady state is called homeostasis, which refers to the set of positive and negative feedback factors that keep the system in a dynamic equilibrium. The steady state may evolve into another steady state over time, but it is protected from strong fluctuations by feedback factors (homeorhesis).

Considering a landscape holistically implies the study of it as a whole rather than focusing only on the functioning of its parts. Such an approach allows the reduction of analytic observations needed to study very complex structures. It rejects the study of separate pieces without connecting them with each other. Because landscape ecology entails the study of the landscape and its many functions in their entirety, it is necessarily multidisciplinary.

The knowledge gained about the relationships among the parts of a landscape and its function as a system can be used as a basis for planning and managing land use. The policy of humans should be to maintain environmental sustainability through stable landscape configurations. Landscapes can be configured to attain human objectives, such as food production. Each configuration affects ecological integrity differently. The character as well as the configuration of the landscape elements determine to a high degree the stability (in the sense of persistence) of the landscape in relation to disturbances to its steady state (Forman, 1989, and private correspondence).

Land use is the varying activities executed by humans to exploit the landscape, such as hunting or ploughing. The land use pattern primarily determines the landscape pattern in areas where land use is intensifying. Therefore, land use patterns may be essential factors in determining landscape stability and should have the attention of land use planners.

The simplest example of manipulating landscape stability by pattern is the contour arrangement of land parcels to prevent soil erosion. Contour ploughing is at the smallest scale of landscape management. At larger scales it is the conservation of permanent vegetation (usually forest) in the water catchment areas of river basins.

More complex is the concept of ecological infrastructure or the importance of connecting landscapes to maintain biodiversity. This concept accepts the necessity of exchange among biological populations. A certain separation is necessary for individual development (evolution). But if the separation becomes complete isolation, because of the fragmentation of landscape due to highly intensive agriculture, it could lead to genetic impoverishment and the extinction of species.

Research on the connectivity of landscapes for groups of species is developing as data on area, distances between patches, stepping stones, and the character of corridors are collected and disseminated. For local planning needs, use can already be made of such knowledge. On a more global scale, the research is less developed. In The Netherlands an attempt has been made to include ecological infrastructure in state land use planning. Implementation is in its early stages. The first steps (on paper) for Europe are in preparation (Benneth, 1991).

More common practices are unplanned extensions of agricultural land that violate the connectivity of landscapes in originally stable ecosystems.

Examples include creating large agricultural or hydrological projects across well-known migratory routes of animals, such as was done to the elephants in Sri Lanka and other animals in Sudan (Cox, 1988). Better examples are the intensification of agricultural production on existing arable land of good quality, optimally using biologically diverse crops. For a real understanding, however, additional research effort and fieldwork will be required.

MEASUREMENT OF LAND USE CHANGE BY REMOTE SENSING

The study of landscapes entails the measurement of land use. The result of human activity is partially seen in the changes in land cover, i.e., the conversion of natural forest to farmland and beaches to urban centers. Measuring these changes involves measuring land cover at different time intervals. Human activity can be measured by asking hunters how many of them are hunting what, when, where, and with what intensity, or by asking farmers what kinds of crops they are cultivating when, where, and how.

Measuring can also be done by assessing the results of human activity, the land cover. This can be observed visually, directly with the eye or by photographs or other remote-sensing methods. Ideally, one would use a combination of measuring the activity and the land cover for each land area of interest.

Measuring land cover is the most suitable type of measurement for global observations. Measuring human activity generally requires more time and energy because visits to the area to be measured and discussions with the people living there are necessary. In administratively and technically advanced countries, statistics are available as well as a series of topographical maps done over time with which to compare the most recent measurements. In less advanced countries, statistics on land use tend to be less accurate and up to date, and topographical mapping is less frequent and of insufficient detail. In these countries, measurement by remote sensing in combination with some fieldwork, to establish the "ground truth," is the only way to come to reasonable results.

In developing countries, assessment of land use over large areas is often difficult without remote sensing. In combination with statistical data, such as those from an agricultural census, and ground truth, remote sensing meets basic land use measurement needs. However, the accuracy of land use classification depends on the scale of the observations, which may be too small (i.e., not much detail) for some planning needs.

The most common means of remote sensing is the use of various wavelengths of electromagnetic radiation. This radiation is reflected from objects on the earth's surface and can be recorded by photography or electronic devices. In all cases, only a limited part of the light spectrum is used.

Infrared radiation is a very useful type of radiation to record because it represents a considerable percentage of the sun's energy that reaches the earth's surface. It is strongly absorbed by water and wet soils and is not used by plants for photosynthesis, so that the energy is reflected by plant tissues to a large extent.

Observations by remote sensing are predominantly made from aircraft for intermediate-scale images. Satellites are used for small-scale images, and very detailed (large-scale) images are taken from fixed platforms, balloons, or small aircraft.

The choice between the various scales and means for remote sensing depends on the nature of the land area, the purpose for the resulting information, and the general economic and political situation (which often determines the availability of data for nonmilitary use). The most universal means for reconnaissance mapping is ordinary black-and-white photography taken at the scale 1:40,000 with a super-wide-angle lens from conventional aircraft.

Interpretation of Remote Sensing Data

The results of the photography and scanning are images that need to be interpreted to transfer the data into usable information. In some cases, special image processing will be done at the same time.

The patterns on a remote-sensing image consist of patches differing in color or gray hue. A most important feature for landscape analysis and classification is the configuration of the pattern elements and how they relate to various types of landscape mosaics. There are random mosaics, regular mosaics like checkerboard ones (sometimes associated with farming), or dot mosaics. These mosaics imply certain ecological infrastructures (Zonneveld, 1988; Forman, 1989; Forman and Godron, 1986).

Essential in photo interpretation is the vertical dimension of the landscape, especially on large or intermediate scales. The large variations in the vertical dimension indicate variations in land relief (e.g., as mountains and oceans), and the smaller variations show the height of ground vegetation. The most important disadvantage of satellite imagery is that vegetation height and low-level land relief are impossible to detect due to the very high altitude from which the images are taken.

Once the various elements on the remote-sensing image have been differentiated into single homogeneous units or, depending on the scale of the image, complexes, then ground truth knowledge is gathered. Stratified sampling is carried out based on the interpretation map of the image, preferably in relatively small representative areas. In this process, various types of land cover on the ground are compared with the image. Surveys, using questionnaires, of functional land use can also be carried out at this stage. Observations from small aircraft can be used to replace ground checks of cover type in areas that are inaccessible. This ground truth is used to more fully interpret the remote-sensing images already gathered (Küchler and Zonneveld, 1988).

Computer-Assisted Interpretation

Since the early days of remote sensing, people have tried to automatize interpretation. The practical possibilities for automation are less than the layman would expect. Nevertheless, the development of electronically recorded remote-sensing images does allow for certain automated classification procedures.

The best opportunities are in areas with large agricultural fields that are easily distinguishable from adjacent areas of natural vegetation. Computer-assisted interpretation is most effective with large homogeneous map elements, such as the U.S. cornfields. Care must be taken in such interpretation because slight differences in superficial structure (roughness, etc.) or temporal changes due to wind or small differences in the growing stages of crops may translate into large differences on the image. In contrast, different crops may appear as the same image. It is particularly difficult to automatize vertical features of landscapes (Kannegieter, 1988; Sombat and van der Zee, 1987).

Use of Remote-Sensing Data

The data collected from land use surveys is used for:

- governmental planning purposes of various kinds,
- commercial assessments of the supply of a land product,
- determining target areas for humanitarian relief efforts, and
- studying environmental degradation and its consequences.

The data should be able to provide answers to the following questions:

- How is the land used?
- How has land use changed?
- What and how much is produced by the land? And
- Who uses the land?

The main constraints in developing countries to utilizing the results of land use surveys are the lack or inaccuracy of statistical (agricultural, cadastral, topographical) data and the irregularity of the land in space and time (i.e., shifting cultivation). Quantitative data on agricultural production are also much more difficult to infer from aerial photographs and satellite imagery than they are in countries like the United States or the former USSR, where large parcels of land with certain spectral signatures allow straightforward calculation. However, in certain regions with characteristic complex land use patterns and distinct growing seasons, it is possible to calculate general data about production potential (Groten, 1991).

An enormous constraint to collecting usable data in many developing countries is the restriction in use of aerial photography due to security reasons. This restriction often necessitates the use of satellite imagery, which, as discussed above, is less detailed than aerial photography.

However, satellite imagery captures large areas in single photos and can be used to distinguish general land use types. Marked differences between official statistics and reality can often be assessed. It is possible, particularly in the dry season, to distinguish between irrigated and nonirrigated agriculture, such as in Sri Lanka and Tunisia. Deforestation can also often be assessed, although it is often difficult to distinguish primary from secondary forests. If seasonal differences exist, however, multitemporal images may provide discrimination possibilities.

In humid tropical zones, it is difficult to obtain sufficiently cloud-free satellite images (Groten, 1991; van der Zee and Cox, 1988). Side Looking Airbourne Radar, which can "look through the clouds," can be used in these areas, but is more expensive (Sicco Smit, 1988). The author's experience in Amazonia revealed that shifting cultivation and coffee plantations can easily be detected on SLAR images.

In most cases, images collected over time are used for monitoring changes in a land area or for "watching in order to warn." For example, such monitoring can point to widespread crop failures. To study seasonal differences, monthly or shorter temporal resolution is required (Groten, 1991). For long-term planning and monitoring, yearly or longer period image collecting is sufficient.

In principle, any land survey method can be used to detect change over time. Compared to a single ad hoc survey, however, costs and compatibility with automation systems are a more important consideration. For this reason, sequential satellite observation has great advantages. It is clear that modern geographic information systems improve considerably the processing and retrieving of sequential survey results.

ACKNOWLEDGMENTS

I am grateful to my ITC colleagues, Dr. S. Groten, Professor N. Mulder, and Dr. D. van der Zee, for their suggestions about and corrections of the content.

REFERENCES

Benneth, G.
  1991 *Towards a European Ecological Network.* The Hague, The Netherlands: Ministry of Agriculture, Nature Management and Fisheries.

Cox, J.A.
  1988 Remote sensing and land evaluation for planning elephant corridors in Sri Lanka. *ITC Journal* 2:172-177.

Forman, R.T.T.
  1982 Interaction among landscape elements: a core of landscape ecology. Pp. 35-48 in S.P. Tjallingii and A.A. de Veer, eds., *Perspectives in Landscape Ecology. Proceedings of the International Congress of the Netherlands Society of Landscape Ecology.* Wageningen, The Netherlands: Centrum voor Landbouwpublikaties en landbouwdocumentatie Wageningen.
  1989 Ecologically sustainable landscapes: the role of spatial configuration. Pp. 261-278 in I.S. Zonneveld and R.T.T Forman, eds., *Changing Landscape: An Ecological Perspective.* New York: Springer-Verlag.

Forman, R.T.T., and M. Godron
  1986 *Landscape Ecology.* New York: John Wiley & Sons.

Groten, S.M.E.
  1991 Satelliten-Montoring von Agrar - Okosystemen im Sahel, (International Institute of Aerial Survey and Earth Science, Enschede, The Netherlands). Inaugural Dissertation, Westfalischen Wiljhelmsuniversitat, Munster, Germany.

Kannegieter, A.
  1988 Mapping land-use. Pp. 335-374 in A.W. Küchler and I.S. Zonneveld, eds., *Vegetation Mapping, Handbook of Vegetation Science.* Dordrecht, The Netherlands: Kluwer Academic Publishers.

Küchler, A.W., and I.S. Zonneveld, eds.
  1988 *Vegetation Mapping, Handbook of Vegetation Science.* Dordrecht, The Netherlands: Kluwer Academic Publishers.

Merriam, G.
  1984 Connectivity: a fundamental ecological characteristic of landscape pattern. Pp. 5-17 in J. Brandt and P. Agger, eds., *Proceedings of the First International Seminar on Methodology in Landscape Ecological Research and Planning.* Denmark: Roskilde University Center.

Sicco Smit, G.
  1988 A practical application of radar imagery for tropical rain forest vegetation mapping. Pp. 249-264 in A.W. Küchler and I.S. Zonneveld, eds., *Vegetation Mapping, Handbook of Vegetation Science.* Dordrecht, The Netherlands: Kluwer Academic Publishers.

Sombat, M., and D. van der Zee
  1987 The monotoring of Bangkok's rural urban fringe. *Ekologiea* 6(1):63-76.

van der Zee, D., and J.A. Cox
  1988 Monitoring in Moneragala district, Sri Lanka. *ITC Journal* 3:260-271.

Zonneveld, I.S.
  1988 Interpretation of remote sensing images. Pp. 65-68 in A.W. Küchler and I.S. Zonneveld, eds., *Vegetation Mapping, Handbook of Vegetation Science.* Dordrecht, The Netherlands: Kluwer Academic Publishers.
  1989 Scope and concepts of landscape ecology as an emerging science. Pp. 1-20 in I.S. Zonneveld and R.T.T. Forman, eds., *Changing Landscape: An Ecological Perspective.* New York: Springer-Verlag.

4

An Ecological Perspective on Population Change and Land Use

Steward T.A. Pickett

Is there a common vocabulary to underwrite studies of population and land use change? Can ecological and social sciences research on the topic be joined? This commentary has three parts. The first concerns the relationship of ecology to the study of human population; the second deals with recent changes in ecology that better dispose it to join with social science research; and the third points out opportunities for interaction between ecology and the social sciences.

American ecology has largely ignored humans. It is unusual in this stance, perhaps due to a combination of factors. First, the vastness of North America, coupled with the frontier mentality, have meant that ecologists have had apparently pristine or lightly human-impacted areas in which to work. But in addition to that opportunity, the dominant ecological world view, or paradigm, has predisposed the American discipline to work with apparently closed, self-regulating systems, for which human effects are external or temporary excursions from a biotic equilibrium. Such an approach reflects the long-lived cultural metaphor of the balance of nature. Yet, despite the dominance of the "equilibrium paradigm," many scholars and scientists have pointed out the error of excluding humans. The battle to include humans in the scope of ecology is evidenced by the persistence of George Perkins Marsh's "great question": "Whether man is of nature or above her?" (Marsh, 1864).

The upstart of this situation is that ecology has, unfortunately, little to say about the subtle effects of human population and its constructions on ecological systems or the ecology of populated areas. But human effects, both subtle and conspicuous, are being increasingly documented at all spatial scales. Geographers, environmental historians, paleoecologists, and landscape ecologists have accumulated an impressive body of information documenting the subtle, indirect, distant, or past effects of human populations throughout the world. The weight, pervasiveness, and ubiquity of the examples have stimulated ecologists to communicate with social scientists and historians. The empirical mass of human effects is beginning to be translated into mainstream ecology.

Ecologists are currently more open to the translation and import of information on human effects because of changes in their own discipline. Empirically, studies of natural disturbances, the extensive migrations of plant and animal species in the past, and studies of climate change force ecologists to see their systems in a different light. As a result, the dominant paradigm is changing in ecology. Ecological systems are now seen by most ecologists as being (1) open to outside influence; (2) often regulated from outside; (3) rarely at or near a single point equilibrium; (4) not strictly deterministic; and (5) inclusive of humans or their effects. This new world view can be called the nonequilibrium paradigm. It suggests a cultural metaphor of "the flux of nature." American ecology is, as a result of the paradigm shift, better prepared to communicate with ecologists in developing countries, whose mandate often causes them to address human population and to communicate with those specialists who study human populations.

An example of recognizing the new frontier in North American ecology is the study of urban rural gradients. Drs. Mark McDonnell, Margaret Carreiro, Richard Pouyat, Gary Lovett, Robert Parmelee, and I have initiated such studies in the New York Metropolitan region (McDonnell and Pickett, 1990). As an introduction into the ecology of this populated area, we wish to know how ecosystem function and forest regeneration are affected by the human population and its environmental effects. Essentially, the specific research questions and approaches are among those that ecologists would apply in any system they chose to study. But we are applying them along a previously neglected axis of environmental contrast. Already we have discovered some new environmental patterns that demand explanation. Although levels of heavy metals in the soil are two to four times higher in urban than rural sites (Pouyat and McDonnell, 1991), and urban soils are highly hydrophobic (White and McDonnell, 1988), the key ecosystem processes of nitrogen mineralization and litter decomposition rates actually increase in urban compared to rural sites (Pouyat et al., n.d.). Ultimately, comparison with other anthropogenic stress and disturbance gradients can expose generalizable and fundamental limits on ecological systems, as well as supply quantitative environmental measurements to evaluate the effects of human population and land use change. Because so many of our treasured natural areas are near the expanding urban fringe, the work promises to have immense practical value as well.

The opportunities for interaction between social science and ecology are great and compelling. The information presented by social scientists at the workshop was at relatively coarse scales. Such scales are critical to understand, predict, and mitigate regional and global effects of human population change. Yet the models and empirical studies presented by the social scientists often used land use patterns as their environmental variable. Such a choice would not connect closely with the work of most ecologists, because the quantifiable environmental variables that are so important to predicting and explaining the workings of ecological systems are almost completely ignored by the focus on land use.

Ecologists can say how the animal populations are regulated, how the communities are distributed in space and time, and how the nutrients and carbon are partitioned and processed in local forest stands, watersheds, or regional landscapes. But the appropriate and important focus of social scientists at the very coarse regional, national, or continental scales resides across a quite broad chasm from most ecology. The two different scales must be bridged by terminology, concepts, measurement techniques, data, models, and ultimately complete theories. From an ecological perspective, the chasm suggests a fundamental question: What are the quantitative environmental effects and biotic consequences of human population and land use change? This question is as important and begging in the United States as in developing countries.

There are two things that social scientists should know about ecology to proceed toward the important interaction with ecologists that can bridge the chasm between human population and land use data and environmental data. One is the structure and intent of modern ecology. I suspect that most established social scientists may have encountered, during their education, a brand of ecology that has been superseded. The classic textbooks from which so many of us were trained took ecology to be strictly the study of the biogeochemistry of ecosystems, or the study of the growth, control, and interaction of populations, or the distribution and limitation of biotic communities. Fortunately, modern ecology is all of these things, along with new bridge disciplines or approaches that hardly existed 20 years ago. Modern ecology is the scientific study of the processes influencing the distribution and abundance of organisms, the interactions among organisms, the interactions between organisms, and the transformation and flux of energy and matter. Within ecology, specialists focus on either distinct entities (e.g., organisms, landscape patch types) or quantitative fluxes (e.g., energy, nutrients) and do so in either a historical and particularist perspective or an instantaneous and ergodic perspective. Furthermore, ecologists can initiate studies by focusing on a particular system or site, or on interactions that

FIGURE 1 The scope of modern ecology showing its shifting but mutual emphasis on abiotic and biotic factors and illustrating the specific disciplines of which ecology is composed. Bordering disciplines are shown in italics.

may range broadly and extend beyond the boundaries of specific systems. The lesson for social scientists is that ecology is not monolithic (Figure 1).

There is a second message for social scientists about ecology. This lesson emerges from comparing the fundamental structure of ecological versus economic development models. These two disciplines represent two great paradigms that reflect radically different assumptions about how systems work. Put most crudely, ecologists, based on their empirical experience at the usual ecological time and space scales, see systems as ultimately limited. This paradigm is reflected in the generalization that no ecological system (organism, population, etc.) grows without limit. Ecological theories are structured around the negative feedbacks and other limits that constrain the basic positive feedback that underlies the growth of systems (Figure 2A; J. Fellows, personal communication, 1991). One basic assumption of economic and development models appear to be that systems are ultimately without limit. Thus, the economic studies and models are cast in terms of overcoming negative feedbacks, and permitting the positive feedbacks to operate without constraint (Figure 2B).

These two great paradigms, the ecological and economic, demand joint analysis. Rather than argue whether, in the universal sense, Malthus was wrong (apparently, an economic conclusion) or right (arguably, a conclusion acceptable to most ecologists when such thinking is applied to their scales and systems), the question should be cast differently. At what temporal and spatial scales, for what parameters, and for what kind of models

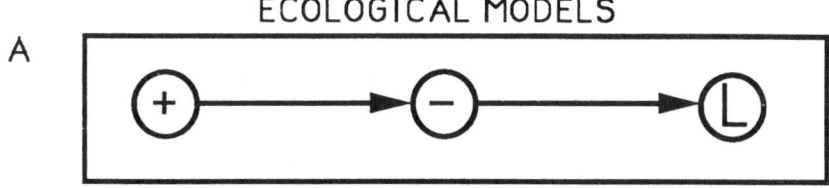

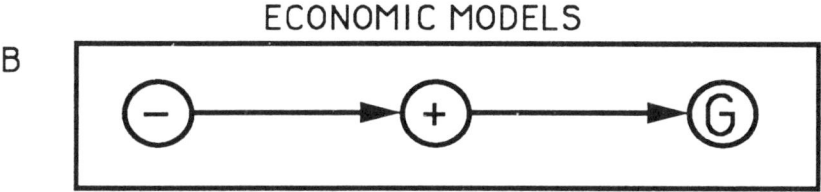

FIGURE 2 Diagram of the fundamental, contrasting form of ecological (A) and economic (B) models. L indicates the assumption that systems are limited, G indicates the assumption of unconfined growth. The "+" sign indicates positive feedback, whereas the "–" sign indicates negative feedbacks and other external limiting factors.

do limits exist or not? What statements in each discipline are meant to be idealizations for guidance of comparison and reference? What ways are there to constrain idealized generalization and expose particular exceptions? Finally, how can slippery but terribly important concepts, such as the quality of human life and the sustainability of ecosystems, be incorporated into the urgent question at the boundary between social and ecological science of whether "man is of nature or above her"?

REFERENCES

Marsh, G.P.
    1864   *Man and Nature: Or Physical Geography as Modified by Human Action.* New York: Scribner.

McDonnell, M.J., and S.T.A. Pickett
    1990   The study of ecosystem structure and function along gradients of urbanization: an unexploited opportunity for ecology. *Ecology* 71:1232-1237.

Pouyat, R.V., and M.J. McDonnell
    1991   Heavy-metal accumulations in forest soils along an urban-rural gradient in southeastern New York, USA. *Water, Air and Soil Pollution* 57-58:797-807.

Pouyat, R.V., M.J. McDonnell, and S.T.A. Pickett
    No date   The effect of urban environments on soil characteristics in oak stands along an urban-rural land use gradient.

White, C.S., and M.J. McDonnell
    1988   Nitrogen cycling processes and soil characteristics in an urban versus rural environment. *Journal of Biogeochemistry* 5:243-262.

5
Northern Nigeria: Land Transformation Under Agricultural Intensification

Michael Mortimore

INTRODUCTION

Objectives

The objective of this case study is to review, in descriptive (rather than explanatory) terms, some evidence on the nature and rate of land transformation processes in two northern Nigerian farming systems. The term "land transformation" (Wolman and Fournier, 1987) is preferred to the more familiar "land use change" because it embraces a broader range of change processes relevant to the population-land equation. A suggested classification of these processes follows:[1]

1. Land use change (the transfer of land from one class of management to another).
2. Land investment (or divestment) in:
   - soil/water conservation structures,
   - irrigation/drainage structures,
   - management structures (especially enclosures),

---

[1] Much more needs to be done before the data and methods can be considered to be satisfactory. In particular, land investment cannot yet be analyzed in quantitative terms, so the discussion of it here is very brief.

- productivity management (especially fertilization), and
- tree planting and protection.
3. Land productivity change in:
    - soil chemical properties,
    - soil physical properties (including moisture),
    - soil biological properties,
    - farm trees—physiognomy (including density and volume), and
    - farm trees—floristic composition.

The term "intensification" is taken to mean the following three interrelated processes:

1. increased frequency of cultivation;
2. labor intensification per hectare; and
3. capital intensification per hectare.

The evidence reported here supports the hypothesis that under conditions of land scarcity, population growth on smallholdings drives agricultural intensification, land investments, and productivity enhancement, which are together consistent with an objective of sustainable resource management.

The Study Area

In the semiarid zone of northern Nigeria (Figure 1), rainfall diminishes northward with the length of the growing season. A vast plain, with local relief rarely exceeding 100 m, slopes gently toward the north and east from about 500 m above sea level at Kano. The soils are predominantly derived from former dune sands and are commonly deep and freely draining. They are low in organic matter, nitrogen, and phosphorus (Jones and Wild, 1975). Restricted areas of interdunal soils have finer textural characteristics, wetter moisture regimes, and sometimes superior organic content. Natural vegetation (now increasingly modified) consists of open thorny savanna woodland and grassland, much influenced by fire, with occasional occurrences of natural grassland on frequently flooded sites or on recently vegetated dunes. Degradation of the soils and vegetation is believed (in official circles) to be widespread, but there are few data (Mortimore, 1989b).

The population densities are very uneven, notwithstanding an appearance of homogeneity in the major environmental variables. There has been no accepted population census since 1963.[2] Population density was last mapped for 1952-1953 (Prothero, 1958). A more recent proxy for population

---

[2]The results of the 1991 census were not available at the time of this writing.

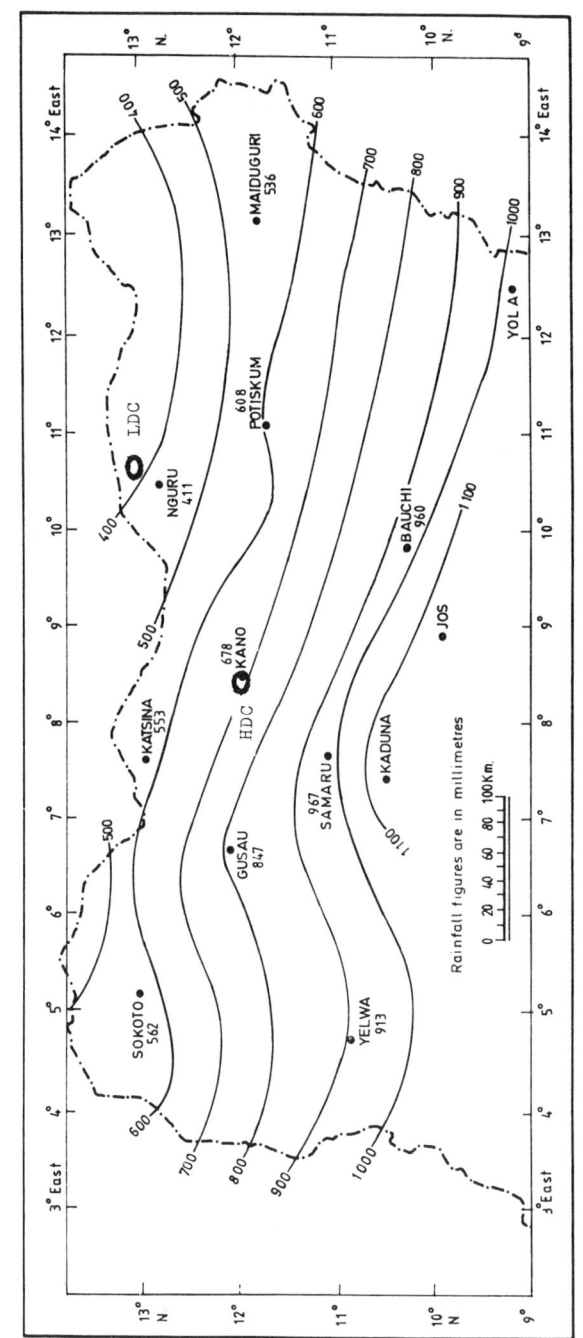

FIGURE 1 Northern Nigeria: average annual rainfall, 1968-1987, showing the locations of study areas. HDC = High-density case; LDC = low-density case. SOURCE: Mortimore (1989b).

density is the percentage of land under cultivation, which was mapped in three classes from a side-looking airborne radar survey in 1977 (Federal Department of Forestry, 1977). This pattern, reduced and generalized, is shown in Figure 2. Such a classification disguises the continuum that exists, from over 80 percent cultivated to zero in uninhabited forest reserves. The lack of census data, or reliable population estimates, for recent years is a handicap in attempting to interpret the process of population change through time.

This chapter presents two case studies that occupy contrasting positions on this continuum. The first is a high-density case (the inner Kano Close-Settled Zone), where rural densities are at least 350 persons/km^2, and the second is a low-density case (the Manga Grasslands), where they are of the order of 100 persons/km^2. The high-density area had an average annual rainfall (1968-1987) of 680 mm and the low-density area averaged 400 mm. More detailed interpretations of ecological and socioeconomic change in these areas are available in Mortimore (1989a, 1993) and Mortimore et al. (1990).

Methods

For estimating land use change over periods of a decade or more, sequential black-and-white air photography has been found to be the only practicable data source, notwithstanding differences in scale, quality, and in the dates of air surveys (though they were always conducted during dry seasons). Very little analysis of land use change has been attempted using the vast air photo resources available in northern Nigeria (but see Field and Collins, 1986). Official land use statistics are based on side-looking airborne radar surveys of 1977 (Federal Department of Forestry, 1977), and for technical reasons, neither this imagery nor earth satellite imagery is fully compatible with air photography. It cannot, therefore, be used as part of a series to evaluate land use change.

The sustainability of a farming system can be assessed from either an economic or an ecological standpoint, but the conservation of the soil resources is a precondition for the longer term continuity of the system. Soil surveys and inventories, however, do not normally address the question of medium-term changes in soil chemical and physical properties, and the need for such monitoring has been neglected (Young, 1993). A recent study has proposed a set of indicators of soil quality and ways of measuring changes caused by management (Larson and Pierce, 1991).

The Central Nigeria Project (Land Resources Development Centre, 1979) carried out extensive soil investigations in the Kano Close-Settled Zone in 1977. Soil pits were dug in catenary sequences at sites representative of major land systems. Profile descriptions, with detailed site and soil de-

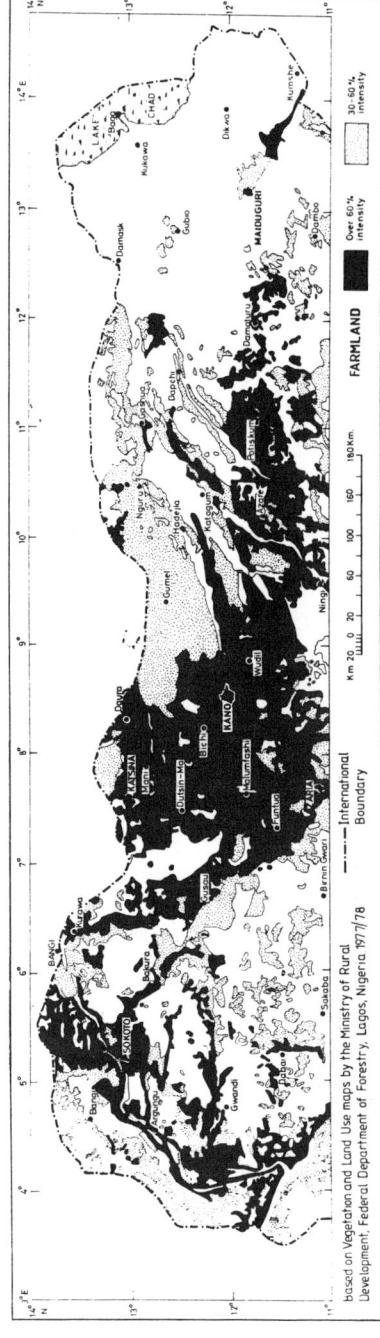

FIGURE 2 Northern Nigeria: intensity of cultivation in 1977, north of latitude 12°N. SOURCE: Mortimore (1989b).

scriptive data, were filed, and samples were taken from representative horizons. Selected samples were analyzed.[3]

For the present study (Mortimore et al., 1990), a selection of catenas, within a radius of 40 km from Kano, was made to represent land systems in the high-density area. New samples of surface soils (0-20 cm) were obtained, by auguring, from sites on the same land facets, and as close as possible to the original soil pits. The new samples were analyzed alongside material from the original samples, using standard analytical procedures. Both original and new samples were obtained from cultivated upland sites. For evaluating change over 13 years (1977-1990), the results were first averaged by catena, then aggregated for each land system, and finally for the whole area of study.[4]

No soil data were available for the low-density area. Studies of the farm tree population in the high-density area used aerial photography of medium scale and three sequential dates, interpreted with stereo equipment and magnified up to 15 times. The air photo work was supplemented with ground surveys in randomly located quadrats, which included species identification, height estimations, and girth measurements of all woody plants above 10 cm in girth at breast height.

POPULATION CHANGE[5]

The High-Density Case

The censuses of 1952 and 1962 suggested a net rate of increase of 2.6-2.9 percent a year (Green, 1970; Mortimore, 1974). Rural rates must have been somewhat lower, because urban rates were 6.7-8.9 percent; 10.5 percent of the Province's population being then urbanized. A demographic survey in Malumfashi (southern Katsina State)—an area of similar ecology—gave a crude rate of natural increase of 2.9 percent for a population of 42,493 in 1973 (Bradley et al., 1982). The general fertility rate (GFR) was 221 per 1,000. In the Nigeria Fertility Survey a decade later (1981/1982), the GFR was reported to be 183 in Kano State, somewhat lower than the Malumfashi estimate.[6] This implies a lower rate of natural increase. Continuing

---

[3]These samples were stored, cataloged, and located on large-scale maps in the Kano Environmental Data Bank at the Department of Geography, Bayero University (McTainsh and Stokes, 1980).

[4]The results of this experiment in longitudinal soil monitoring are regarded as provisional, in view of the small number of samples analyzed and the limitations of the method.

[5]In the absence of census data for the last three decades, population change has to be inferred from fragmentary information.

[6]The Nigeria Fertility Survey defined the GFR as the number of children born per 1,000 women aged 15 to 49 in the 5-year period before the survey. The figure may be low owing to inaccurate recall.

high rates of infant mortality and a deterioration in public health care delivery during the past decade are widely believed to have affected rural areas in the semiarid zone of Nigeria. It is quite possible, therefore, that the rate of natural increase is well below the national average (estimated to be 3.3 percent in the World Bank's projections based on the early 1980s [World Bank, 1984]).[7]

Migration is difficult to measure, even at the microlevel. There is also a great deal of seasonal and short-term circulation, which fluctuates from year to year.

Translated into density, the available information suggests an average density of 235 persons/km^2 in the Close-Settled Zone (Ungogo District) in 1962,[8] and in three villages surveyed in 1964, 353 persons/km^2 (Mortimore and Wilson, 1965). Given a cultivated ratio of 84 percent, the amount of arable land per head was 0.24 ha in these villages and 0.36 ha in the District. Any subsequent estimate of density is speculative. If the rate of natural increase after 1962 were assumed to be 2.9 percent (as in Malumfashi in 1973), and migration were zero, the average density in Ungogo District in 1988 would have been 495 persons/km^2 — an increase that is improbable on the basis of field observation. If, on the other hand, out-migration is assumed to have averaged 1.5 percent, a resulting net increase of 1.4 percent would have generated a density of 347 persons/km^2 by 1990. This would allow 0.24 ha of arable land per head, only 68 percent of what was available in 1962.

The Low-Density Case

Very little information is available for the low-density study area. It can be safely assumed that the rate of natural increase does not exceed 2.9 percent (the Malumfashi estimate). Out-migration is probably considerable, even when seasonal and short-term circulation is excluded. Net population growth may therefore be as low as 1 percent. Some support for such an assumption is provided by the example of Dagaceri village, where the number of households did not change significantly between 1975 and 1986 (Mortimore, 1989a:98). Dagaceri lies outside the Manga Grasslands, but is ethnically, culturally, and ecologically comparable. Market towns, on the

---

[7]In the inner Kano Close-Settled Zone, growth rates apparently fell from 2.2 percent in 1931-1952 to 1.2 percent in 1952-1962, probably as the result of out-migration. Hill (1977:91-92) estimated an average net increase of only 1 percent from 1932 to 1971 in Kumbotso District.

[8]The cancelled census of 1962 is considered, on the basis of limited field checks, to be more reliable in Kano than the published census of 1963.

other hand, may grow rapidly. There is also some local redistribution of the population, including occasional resettlement, on new sites, of entire villages.

According to the 1952 census, the districts of Bornu Province in which the Manga Grasslands then lay had population densities in the range of 20-50 persons/km^2. The average density now is thought not to exceed 100 persons/km^2.

The Demographic Basis of Intensification

Rising population densities—at opposite ends of the range—provide the potential for labor intensification in the farming systems. A longitudinal review of the evidence available follows.

A comparison between the two areas, whose present densities differ by a factor of 4, provides an opportunity to test the hypothesis that population density is a predictor of agricultural intensification. Such an investigation is, however, complicated by ecological and historical differences—no two areas can be strictly comparable. The high- and low-density areas represent different points on the rainfall gradient, have different soils and topography, and are differently located with respect to precolonial political and commercial centers.

LAND USE CHANGE

The High-Density Case

In 1964, 79.6 percent of the area was under upland (rainfed) cultivation, and an additional 4.2 percent was irrigated lowland (Mortimore and Wilson, 1965). Cultivated upland was under annual cropping with sorghum, millet (*Pennisetum typhoides*), cowpeas (grown in mixtures), and groundnuts (grown in mixtures or alone in rotations). Farmyard manure was applied at an average rate of 4.1 tons/ha, but ranging from 0 to 6.5 on individual holdings. The average size of fields was 0.5-1.0 ha, and of holdings, 1.76 ha (range: <1 to >10 ha).

Land preparation (for groundnuts only), planting, weeding (three times), and harvesting were accomplished with labor-intensive hand hoes and machetes. Fields were permanently divided by living boundaries of thatching grass, useful shrubs, and trees. Farm trees were distributed irregularly in the cultivated fields at densities of 12-15/ha, and produced marketable output, construction and craft materials, and food. Fallows only occurred when a household was unable to cultivate its holding fully, for example through illness. Such holdings provided both the basis of household subsistence and a marketable surplus (groundnuts). There were active markets in land and labor, with rising prices for both.

Shrub- or grassland-occupied low-lying sites were considered unsuitable for cultivation on account of flooding and were heavily grazed and cut over. Some erosion occurred on the banks of streams.

This land use system had evolved over a period of many centuries and was quite stable. Aerial photography done in 1981 indicates that, after 18 years, the only significant change to have occurred was the transfer of some cultivated land to residential and commercial development. Average rainfall, and possibly flood risk, had diminished by over 25 percent since the 1960s.

An analysis of land use change in an area of 332 km^2 between 1965-1966 and 1981 confirms this conclusion (Table 1). A reduction in the area of flood plain, as interpreted from the photographs, after 1971 was due to the drying out of the soils during several successive years of drought.

The expansion of cultivation, therefore, reached its conclusion several decades ago, with fallows virtually eliminated on the upland. Fieldwork in 1990 suggests that small areas of shrubland, notwithstanding their poor quality, had been added to the cultivated upland. Multicropping is still restricted to lowland sites (though pumps have increased the lift available) and by the water supply.

This stable land use pattern, however, disguises important changes in the farming system (Mortimore, in press). (a) Until inorganic fertilizers became available, there was a long-term decline in yields. Data limitations do not permit this decline to be measured. (b) There is better evidence of a long-term decline in the average size of holdings through subdivision on inheritance (for example, see Mortimore, 1967). (c) There is incontrovertible evidence of manifold increases in the prices paid for land. (d) House-

TABLE 1 Percentage Land Use Change, High-Density Case, 1965-1981

Land Use	1965-1966	1971	1981
Cultivated upland	87.12	86.73	85.46
Cultivated and uncultivated floodplain	8.64	10.08	5.95
Settlement	1.21	1.71	4.85
Eroded area	2.70	0.88	2.22
Others	0.33	0.60	1.52
Total	100.00	100.00	100.00
Area mapped (km^2)	332	365	435
Scale of photography	1:40,000	1:40,000	1:25,000

SOURCE: Mortimore et al. (1990).

hold grain insufficiency is socially extensive and may plausibly have increased. (e) Inputs of farmyard manure increase with population density (Hill, 1986) and inorganic fertilizer inputs increased from the 1960s to the 1980s. (f) Labor hiring has increased in cost and probably also in occurrence. (g) An increasing percentage of farmers use ox-ploughs, though the percentage varies between districts (from 28 to 69 percent according to official figures). The proportion was very small in the 1960s. Although a labor-saving technology, the ox-plough is associated with intensification (Boserup, 1965; Pingali et al., 1987). (h) Groundnuts, after being destroyed by rosette disease in 1975, ceased to be a major crop, and a high-yielding cowpea introduced by the World Bank's integrated rural development authority was taken up in the 1980s. (i) Livestock ownership (most commonly small ruminants, but including some cattle) continues to be very widespread and highly valued. There is no evidence of livestock ownership declining, though numbers fluctuate in response to the primary perception of animals as realisable assets, in particular when drought occurs (Mortimore et al., 1990).

The Low-Density Case

The upland subsystem consists of homogeneous, freely draining sands in a hummocky terrain of stabilized dunes, easily remobilized when the vegetation is removed. This vegetation is grassland, dominated by the annual, *Cenchrus biflorus*, which provides good year-round grazing. Settlements are sited on the upland, often in association with overgrazed and degraded patches. The lowland subsystem contains all the natural woodland (dominated by the dum palm, *Hyphaene thebaica*) and, where depressions intersect the water table, seasonal or permanent saline lakes. They support all the irrigated and most of the rainfed cultivation.

Rainfed millet (*Pennisetum typhoides*), intercropped with cowpeas, provides the basis of household subsistence. Apart from irrigated plots, cultivated land is rotated in cycles of several years' annual cultivation, followed by rest periods of 10 years or more. There is no systematic use of farmyard manure, though livestock may be coralled on the fields. Field and holding sizes are at least double those of the high-density area, and planting densities, one-half or less. Planting is done in unprepared land, two weedings are accomplished with a labor-saving hoe (the *ashasha*), field boundaries are usually unmarked, and farm trees are extremely sparse. Fallows are occupied by regenerating dum palm bush and grasses.

The data in Table 2 show that between 1950 and 1969 the land use system was relatively stable,[9] with the exception of the loss of some wood-

---

[9]When the study was done, no more recent photographs were available. Updating to 1991 will shortly be carried out with new photographs.

TABLE 2 Percentage Land Use Change, Low-Density Case, 1950-1969

Terrain Type	Land Cover Class	1950	1969
Upland		67.8	71.8
	Grassland	66.3	70.3
	Woodland	0	0.1
	Cultivation	0.3	0.5
	Settlement	0.3	0.1
	Mobile sand	0.9	0.8
Lowland		32.2	28.2
	Grassland (sparsely wooded)	2.9	3.7
	Open woodland	13.1	10.7
	Dense woodland	4.3	3.3
	Cultivation (lightly wooded)	9.9	7.9
	Lake beds	2.0	2.6
Total		100.0	100.0
Area mapped (km^2)		1,500	1,500
Scale of photography		1:30,000	1:40,000

SOURCE: Mortimore (1989a).

land. This was converted to grassland. The cultivated area appears not to have increased.[10] The small extent of change in the areas of cultivation and settlement conflict with expectations based on a high assumed rate of population growth during the period.

Field studies indicate that the most visible change to occur since 1969 was an increase in the extent of mobile sand, which by 1986 had come to occupy up to 20 percent of one or two badly affected localities. This increase is attributed to the effects of drought and reduced rainfall more than to management, since the evidence available on livestock numbers does not indicate a substantial increase, and cultivation is not generally associated with dune remobilization (Mortimore, 1989a).

Land Use Change and Population Growth

Land use change in the high-density area is no longer significant (except for the expansion of settlements and the effects of hydrological change).

---

[10]The apparent decrease should be treated with caution. The figures are subject to error and too much should not be read into small changes in small categories.

Intensification trends in the low-density area, an expected extension of the cultivated area, in accordance with the demographic trend, was not detected on the aerial photographs taken from 1950 to 1969. This stability may be explained by one of two hypotheses:

(1) that the upland subsystem is unsuitable for rainfed cultivation in most years and that cultivable land is restricted largely to the lowland subsystem; or

(2) that net population increase was brought to a stop by out-migration and that the subsequent labor shortage impeded further expansion of cultivation.

Comparison of the two systems shows that the low-density area lacks all the evidence of intensification noted in the high-density area, with the exception of irrigated/flood retreat/perennial farming, for which there is a shortage of suitable sites.

LAND INVESTMENT

Introduction

If capital is scarce, investments in the productivity of smallholder farming systems must use family or community-based labor inputs in addition to those necessary to produce a current output. Inadequate inputs, in new investments or in maintaining investments, may cause a loss of productive capacity. It is implicit in theories that attempt to explain land degradation in terms of smallholder mismanagement that divestment, not investment, occurs, because the investment created by initial clearance, enclosure, etc., is subsequently lost. But if the population is growing, such an outcome seems inconsistent with an increasing supply of labor (unless there is a net transfer of labor out of agriculture). To maintain or improve its productivity, a growing population must invest in, not divest, its land.

At the level of the household, because of family fission and the subdivision of holdings, inadequate output may be perceived as being due to a shortage of land rather than a growing population. It is obvious that failure to invest in land improvement threatens not only current output but also the resources of the next generation.

In northern Nigeria, the importance of community-based labor has declined relative to that of hired labor. Labor-intensive agricultural practices and investments on smallholdings therefore take place as a result of access to capital as well as to labor. Notwithstanding this complicating factor, there is a simple association between visible farm investment and high population density, as the case studies show. In the following account, no quantification is attempted.

Soil and Water Conservation Structures

In the high-density area, substantial sheetwash occurs on cultivated land after heavy rain, notwithstanding average slopes of less than 3°, and gullies are common near incised river channels and on steeper slopes. The soils have a tendency to capping, where left uncultivated. Nevertheless, deep cultivable soil horizons, along with little government interest in controlling soil erosion (even in colonial times—compared with East Africa), gave a low profile to soil and water conservation in smallholder perceptions. Investments in water conservation are minimal.

In the low-density area, wind, not water is the main agent of erosion. Where dune remobilization threatens lowland farms or date plantations, attempts may be made to construct barrier fences. These rarely succeed, and both villages and farms may be slowly overwhelmed. Soil conservation or stabilization structures are not attempted on grazing land.

Irrigation

Given a unimodal rainfall regime, and short growing seasons, multicropping depends on irrigation, which is an old, established technology. The hand-operated water lift is constructed entirely from local materials, and the banks, canals, and drains may likewise be created entirely by labor, though nowadays this is often hired.

In the high-density area, this older, labor-intense technology is now giving way to purchased petrol pumps and flexible pipes. Irrigated crops (principally vegetables) grown in the lowlands have always been directed largely to the market. Land, labor, and input markets as well as marketing channels organized by middlemen are therefore characteristic of the sector. Access to irrigated farms (which may be as small as 0.1 ha) is widely sought and there is not enough land, or water, to meet the demand. Before the advent of the petrol pump, prodigious efforts might be made to extend the height or distance range of hand-lifted irrigation water. Such farms also support many fruit trees. They represent the apex of the investment process in smallholder farming—often originally created by family labor but now increasingly financed.

In the low-density area, irrigable land is only found on the banks of saline lakes in topographical depressions. A variety of crops are produced for local markets. Pumps have not been introduced, and might draw down the water table if they were. Lowland sites are more commonly used for flood-retreat cultivation or perennials like sugar. The presence of irrigated multicropping in this low-density area is significant. With only 9-10 percent of the area under cultivation, compared with over 80 percent in the high-density area, farm labor is less scarce than the low population density (<100 persons/km^2) might suggest.

Enclosures

In the high-density area, irrigated farms must be enclosed by animal-proof fences, because their greatest activity takes place during the dry season, when customary grazing rights are unrestricted. Upland farms that are used for cassava (which remains in the ground throughout the year) must also be enclosed, characteristically by earth banks 1 m high surmounted by living or cut branch fences. Other upland farms are permanently bounded, not to control animals, but to demarcate holdings and as productive investments—perennial thatching grasses (e.g., *Andropogon gayanus*), shrubs with marketable products (e.g., *Lawsonia inermis*), or useful trees (e.g., *Parkia biglobosa*). Such boundaries often remain unchanged for more than a generation. Oriented in a rectangular grid facing Mecca, they define the characteristic visible structure of the landscape. Intensive livestock production is now creating a new need, on farms belonging to wealthy individuals, for purchased wire fences. Notwithstanding customary free grazing, exclusive rights may be asserted without dispute. This underlines that tenurial arrangements must not conflict with land investments.

In the low-density area, only irrigated fields, and those under perennials, are enclosed or even marked with visible boundaries. Individual fields may extend to several hectares, and bounding landmarks (trees, breaks of slope) are sufficiently exact to define ownership.

Fertilization

The use of farmyard manure in the high-density area has been considered above. Made from mixing penned livestock dung with ash, uneaten crop residues, and domestic waste, it is distributed to the fields by donkey, cart, or (recently) by motor pickups, and placed by hand around the growing stands. This work is labor intensive. Residues may also be burnt in the fields. Inorganic fertilizers were accepted first for the market crop (groundnuts) because this investment could not be created by labor only. Fertilization is primarily directed toward current output. But farmers recognize the residual effects of manure, and the need to maintain a regime over the years. Supply is limited by the size of livestock holdings; those who can afford to, purchase manure. Because this may contain much unwanted city refuse, still more labor must be given to sorting and burning it. Neither the rising price of manure nor the value (opportunity cost) of labor have deterred farmers from continuing to invest heavily in this form of land improvement. In the low-density area, there is none, except by grazing or night-coralled livestock.

Trees

In the high-density area, a dense scatter of multipurpose trees is found on almost all farms. These represent useful selections from the natural flora (e.g., *Adansonia digitata*), imported exotics from other ecological zones or countries (e.g., *Parkia biglobosa, Mangifera indica*), or species promoted by the Forest Department (e.g., *Azadirachta indica*). The planting and protection of such trees is an old, established practice in the farming system, and they are managed for the production of a range of foods, medicines, fodder, industrial materials, and fuel (Cline-Cole et al., 1990).

In the low-density area, trees (especially date palms) are found on lowland farms in considerable numbers, but on cultivated upland sites, where the water table is deep, only occasional volunteers from the natural flora are found.

Investment and Population Growth

Comparison of the farming systems in the high- and low-density areas indicates that labor investment in improved farm productivity is associated with high population density (or scarcity of land), and not with low density (or relative abundance of land); that it has intensified with time as the population has grown in the high-density area; and that high labor investment is associated with increased financial flows as the market expands. Irrigation investment is primarily market-driven, and the increasing use of hired, as opposed to family or community-based labor, exposes the limit of the demographic hypothesis of land use change in this regard.

In the low-density area, the only significant investments are on lowland farms alongside permanent water sources, where the natural scarcity of sites simulates the overall scarcity of land in the high-density area. But here also, markets influence investment.

SOIL MANAGEMENT[11]

Soil Physical Properties

Table 3 summarizes the data on bulk density and particle size of cultivated upland soils in the high-density area. With regard to bulk density, the

---

[11]Data on changes in soil properties over time are only available for the high-density area.

TABLE 3 Soil Physical Properties, High-Density Area, 1977-1990

Property	1977	1990
Bulk density (gm/m^3)	1.38	1.40
Particle size distribution (%)		
Coarse sand (>177 µ)	26	23
Fine sand (74-177 µ)	55	61
Very fine sand (50-73 µ)	9	7
Silt (2-49 µ)	6	6
Clay (<2 µ)	4	4
Number of catenas	16	16
Number of samples	59	59

SOURCE: Mortimore et al. (1990)

differences between the values for 1977 and those for 1990 are not significant. With regard to particle size distribution, the overall results suggest a small diminution in the coarse sand fraction, an increase in the predominant fine sand fraction, a small increase in very fine sand, and no significant changes in the silt and clay fractions, each being less than 7 percent. The cultivation technologies are not known, but except for one land system, the soils show little evidence of physical deterioration under long-term annual cultivation.

Soil Chemical Properties

Table 4 summarizes the data on soil chemical properties in 1977 and 1990. The values obtained for organic carbon indicate overall a 14 percent decline (varying from a 25 percent decrease in one land system to an 11 percent increase in another). Rates of change between 1 and 2 percent per year are suggested. On the land system where carbon is lowest, it appears to be most stable, and on the land system where it is highest, it is declining most rapidly.

For total nitrogen, an increase is indicated, ranging in the land systems from 4 to 23 percent (less than 2 percent per year).

The evidence for a fall in cation exchange capacity is restricted to one land system. There are no differences in the average values obtained for calcium and magnesium. The drop in the values obtained for potassium was mostly confined to one land system. The increase in sodium is not considered to be significant. The differences in soil pH are also insignificant.

TABLE 4 Soil Chemical Properties, High-Density Case, 1977-1990

Property	1977	1990	% Change
Organic carbon (%)	0.237	0.205	−14
Total nitrogen (%)	0.029	0.033	14
Cation exchange capacity (me%)	2.4	2.2	-8
Exchangeable calcium (me%)	1.5	1.5	0
Exchangeable magnesium (me%)	0.9	0.9	0
Exchangeable potassium (me%)	0.1	0.06	−40
Exchangeable sodium (me%)	0.15	0.16	7
Soil pH, water	5.9	6.1	3
Number of catenas	16	16	
Number of samples	59	59	

NOTE: me% = milliequivalents %.

SOURCE: Mortimore et al. (1990).

The average values cover a lot of variability among land systems and catenas. For the sample as a whole, there is insufficient evidence to demonstrate a one-way trend in any of the properties.

Comparison of Cultivated with Uncultivated Soils

It might be expected that soils under long-term annual cultivation in such a climate would, if stable, be much less fertile than uncultivated soils—having arrived at a low-level equilibrium. To test this possibility, two catenas sampled in the earlier study, one inside a forest reserve and one outside it on cultivated farmland, were resampled. Comparing these soils with one another, and those of the forest reserve with those on farmland in the Close-Settled Zone, does not support the hypothesis that the properties of cultivated upland soils are of a lower order of magnitude than those of uncultivated soils in a comparable ecological zone. The uncultivated soils are affected by compaction, loss of finer soil fractions, a decline in total nitrogen and (commonly) of organic carbon, generally all of which are greater than in the cultivated soils of the Close-Settled Zone during the same period. However, it should be noted that the forest reserve is under extremely heavy grazing pressure.

Fertilization

Samples of organic manure have been found to contain 0.5 percent nitrogen, 0.3 percent phosphorus, 0.7 percent potassium, 1.3 percent cal-

TABLE 5 Illustrative Rates of Nutrient Application

Treatment	Nutrients/ha (kg)				
	N	P	K	Mg	Ca
Organic manure					
2.5 ton/ha	280	168	393	725	393
6 ton/ha	672	402	942	1,742	942
12 ton/ha	1,344	804	1,884	3,480	1,884
Crop residues					
Field residues, 1.3 ton/ha	3	162	55	NA	NA
Roots, 0.7 ton/ha	1	132	67	NA	NA
Total, 2 ton/ha	4	296	122	NA	NA

NOTE: N = nitrogen; P = phosphorus; K = potassium; Mg = magnesium; Ca = calcium; and NA indicates data not available.

SOURCE: Mortimore et al. (1990).

cium, and 0.7 percent magnesium (Essiet, personal communication). Smaller quantities of some nutrients are added to the soil in the form of residues and roots that are swept and dug up at the end of the dry season and burnt. The average weight of field residues in a 5 × 5 m quadrat was found to be 3.3 kg, and of roots of sorghum and millet, 1.8 kg. These values are equivalent to 1.3 and 0.7 tons/ha respectively, containing up to 0.5 percent nitrogen, and significant quantities of phosphorus and potassium (up to 3,800 ppm and 1900 ppm, respectively). Table 5 shows illustrative rates of nutrient application (based on fragmentary data). The inputs illustrated here take no account of animal droppings in the fields, leaf litter, or burnt prunings and other farm detritus; neither do they take account of variability in the nutrient content of different types of organic manure.

Soil Management and Population Density

Evidence has been presented that the topsoils on cultivated upland in the high-density area are stable with respect to most of the standard diagnostic physical and chemical soil properties. Although the values tend to accord with low levels of fertility, a comparison with uncultivated soils suggests that the soils are by no means degraded. The maintenance of fertility is the prime objective of smallholder soil management. If, as this conclusion implies, soil fertility decline can be stabilized under a high and increasing population density, then agricultural intensification is compatible with ecological sustainability in the farming system.

By contrast, in the low-density area soil fertility levels (perhaps comparable to those of the high-density area) are maintained by long fallow cycles, and population growth has not yet forced a transition to more intensive methods of fertility maintenance, even though about 70 percent of the area is usually excluded from farming use.

FARM TREES

Under a regime of annual cultivation, natural woodland is gradually transformed, by the clearance, selection, protection, and planting of trees, into farmed parkland. The trees provide, among their many functions, browse for small ruminants in an integrated system of crop, livestock, and tree husbandry. Under such conditions, the density, volume, and regenerative status of the tree stock is a measure of sustainability in the system. Under less intensive systems, the tree stock responds to population growth in different ways, because natural vegetation is more abundant.

The High-Density Area

Studies of farm tree populations in two areas (west and east of Kano), using sequential aerial photography and ground surveys, generated the data summarized in Table 6.

Notwithstanding the differences between the values obtained for the two areas, the table shows that the farmed parkland has been sustained over three decades including two major drought cycles (1972-1974 and 1983-1984). In the western area, the density of trees actually increased between 1972 and 1981. In both areas, the ground quadrats surveyed for the wood volume estimates (in 1985 and 1990) exceeded, on average, the densities obtained from aerial photography (1981). This may be due to a further increase in the numbers of trees or the inclusion of saplings not visible on the photographs.

The girth classes of trees (Table 7), taking all species together, indicate that a large proportion of the tree population belongs to the smaller classes, showing that regeneration is taking place (though the distributions are strikingly different in the two areas). However, some species are doing better than others.

The Low-Density Area

Trees are very sparse on rainfed farms. Woodfuel, construction timber, and other products are obtained from natural woodlands in the uncultivated lowlands. Trees are sometimes regarded as a nuisance on farms as they may harbor bird pests. They have not, therefore, been integrated into the

TABLE 6 Tree Densities and Wood Volume, High-Density Area

Method	Year	West	Year	East
Air photo interpretation				
Sampled area (km^2)		2.03		5.3-6.4
Density (trees/ha)	1965-66	NA		7.2
	1972	10.0		7.3
	1981	12.3		7.3
Ground survey				
Sampled area (ha)	1985	94	1990	31
Density (trees/ha)		22.0		11.5
Wood volume (m^3/ha)^a		12.4		19.6
Size of area (km^2)		170		311

NOTE: NA indicates data not available.

^{a}The estimates of wood volume are notional, being based on girth at breast height and using the volume of a cylinder, a formula that has not been tested empirically in this ecological system.

SOURCES: Data from J. Nichol, in Cline-Cole et al. (1990); Mortimore et al. (1990).

farming system (with the exception of the date palm, which is grown on plantations on well-watered lowland sites). Neither have livestock, which spend the greater part of the year on natural grassland, only visiting the farms when crop residues are available.

Farm Trees and Population Density

In northern Nigeria (and elsewhere in West Africa), the transition from bush fallowing to annual cultivation (normally associated with increasing population density) leads to an increase in the size of trees and in timber volume per hectare (Cline-Cole et al., 1990; Pullan, 1974). In the high-density area, the density and regenerative status of farm trees has been maintained over a period of three decades including two major drought cycles. The value and multiple uses of farm trees have ensured this outcome, notwithstanding inflating woodfuel prices in nearby Metropolitan Kano. Increased integration of farm forestry with crop and livestock husbandry is essential to the process of intensification and is consistent with an increasing density of population.

In the low-density area, a lower level of integration and an underdeveloped farm forestry component reflect a lower population density (a more

TABLE 7 Percentages of Girth Size Classes of Farm Trees, High-Density Area

Class (GBH in m)	Area	
	West	East
0.0-0.19	32	NA
0.2-0.39	17	NA
0.4-0.59	10	NA
0.6-0.79	7	NA
0.8-0.99	8	NA
Subtotal	74	48
1.0-1.9	NA	33
2.0-2.9	NA	11
3.0-3.9	NA	4
≥4.0	NA	4
Subtotal	26	52
Total	100	100

NOTE: GBH = girth at breast height. NA indicates data not available by class.

SOURCES: J. Nichol, in Cline-Cole et al. (1990); Mortimore et al. (1990).

abundant supply of land), more natural woodland (on lowland sites), and also ecological constraints affecting the growth of trees in upland areas.

DEMOGRAPHIC VERSUS NONDEMOGRAPHIC FACTORS

The evidence reviewed so far leads to the conclusion that population growth, and high population density, are compatible with sustainable resource management by smallholders. A relationship between population growth and agricultural intensification in northern Nigeria could be inferred long before Ester Boserup's elegant statement of her hypothesis in 1965.[12]

A review of the farming system of the high-density case (the Kano Close-Settled Zone), during the last three decades, concluded that it is sustainable as a system (Mortimore, in press). We may now add that intensifi-

---

[12]The relationship is implicit if not explicitly stated in early colonial annual reports and district assessment reports for Kano Province, for example, and even in the accounts of nineteenth-century explorers. For an early formal statement, see Grove (1961).

cation appears to promote sustainable management of soil and farm tree resources.

Ecological variation, while complicating the spatial pattern, lends further credence to the demographic hypothesis in the sense that highly productive land (usually lowland) is relatively scarce in relation to less productive land (upland), and thus in greater demand. Scarcity has the same effect as a high population, and so consequently many of these areas have been invested in and intensively used, even under relatively low population densities.

The link between population growth and sustainable intensification is mediated by other factors that can only be briefly touched on here.

Land appropriation (by governments, institutions, and capitalist farmers) proceeded apace in Nigeria under the impetus of oil revenues and the making of personal fortunes in the 1970s and 1980s (Watts, 1987). Access to land is facilitated by a land law that accords separate status to customary and statutory tenure, almost unrestricted powers to state governments' land offices to effect transfers, and by subeconomic rates of compensation paid to customary claimants. The removal of increasing amounts of land, cultivated or uncultivated, from the stock available to the growing population of smallholders, may be expected to accelerate the effects of population growth on the use of what remains. There is also a process of purchase, consolidation, and enlargement under customary tenure, which operates in favor of an emerging class of farmer entrepreneurs (Labaran, 1987), which is also reported on irrigation schemes. In short, a process of competitive appropriation is increasingly affecting the supply and distribution of agricultural land.

A further limitation of the demographic hypothesis of land use change arises from the fact that population growth does not translate directly into increased inputs of agricultural labor. At the level of the household, differences in access to land cause unevenness in family labor inputs. The hiring market either corrects or accentuates such unevenness, depending on the distribution of operating capital and of household poverty within the community. Capital may be spent on hiring labor or on saving it (e.g., by buying ox-plows). This technology has contradictory effects in densely populated areas, saving labor in land preparation but creating extra demand for it in hand-weeding operations.

Actual family labor inputs are also influenced by their opportunity costs in alternative income earning activities, at home or away; by the sexual division of labor; by labor withdrawal for education; and by random indisposition. Among these, the opportunity costs seem to be crucial. Thus the extent of a household's dependence on homegrown food cannot really be described. It is a function of the structure of alternative opportunities open to the individuals within it. If off-farm activity offers a better perceived return than labor invested in subsistence production, the link between population growth and land use is no longer inevitable.

Markets are not new to northern Nigeria. The Kano Close-Settled Zone produced grain for the precolonial city of Kano, and the commercial value of lowland was recognized in a special tax. Farmers might earn incomes as laborers, craftsmen, or traders, especially during the dry season. The precolonial economy of the Manga Grasslands was based in part on the production and sale of potash and salt from saline lake beds. Livestock were also bought and sold. Markets were linked by long-distance trading networks, and both local and travelling traders operated in rural areas.

Export crop production (groundnuts and cotton in particular) added to the demand for land, because households maintained a subsistence priority, though by the 1960s, land-poor producers in Kano had to sacrifice a part of their grain output to participate in the groundnut market. Since the demise of the groundnut as an export crop (in 1975), its place has been taken (to a large extent) by grain production for urban markets. In lowland irrigation in particular, market development has an important impact. In a study of *fadama* (lowland) use in nearly 19,000 km^2, Turner (1977) found that distance to markets had a strong correlation with the proportion cultivated. But the next most important variable was settlement density, a proxy for population density. The penetration of markets into the farming sector has received added impetus from inflationary food prices, especially during the last decade. Markets for produce, inputs, working capital, land, and labor, all affect agricultural activity to an increasing extent, even in areas remote from towns.

Market growth and population growth were linked in Boserup's (1965) statement of the demographic hypothesis. Land transformation is tied to both. The extent to which it correlates with changing population density (apparently independent of market influence) is attributable to the continuing priority accorded by peasant smallholders to household subsistence production. This, it is well known, is related to risk. Risk comes from the unpredictable operation of ecological factors (especially rainfall) and of the political economic environment. Our study areas are marginal with respect to both.

CONCLUSIONS

Two farming systems in semiarid Nigeria—high- and low-density cases—that have population growth rates probably lying between 1.5 and 3.0 percent per year, represent two different points in the process of land transformation. These points have cultivated percentages of over 80 in the high-density case and about 10 in the low. Smallholder investment in land improvement is relatively far advanced in the high-density case and has barely begun in the low (except for moisture-rich lowland sites). Soil fertility is being managed on a sustainable basis on the permanent fields of the high-density case, whereas in the low-density case, long fallows are relied on. The farm tree component of the high-density system—well integrated with crops and livestock—is also being managed sustainably, whereas farm trees do not play a significant part in the low-density system, except on lowland sites. It is concluded that population growth, and high population density, are compatible with sustainable resource management under smallholder conditions.

The evidence on soil fertility and farm tree management in the high-density case is derived from small samples, restricted to one farming system, and the conclusions derived from it are provisional. Nevertheless, they challenge the view, commonly held, that population growth necessarily puts destructive pressure on smallholder farming systems, and especially the rapid rates of growth that have been experienced in the last two decades.

Growing population density may take expression, in a farming system in which smallholders aim to produce a large proportion of their subsistence, in either an intensification or a degradation pathway. What Lele and Stone (1989) call "autonomous intensification" has been proceeding in northern Nigeria for decades, and there is a case for "policy-led intensification" to consolidate the gains, and to minimize the possibilities for degradation.

But the threshold for a transition from a degradational to an intensification pathway (the possibility of which was recognized three decades ago by Prothero, 1962) is not clearly understood owing to the shortage of empirical studies. Figure 3 (which is illustrative) suggests that irreversible degradation (frequently asserted in the literature about semiarid Africa) may be more accurately portrayed as a low-level equilibrium, under which economic yields, however scanty, continue. The high-density case, based on the evidence presented here, represents either stable intensification (no degradation and no yield improvement) or improving intensification (sustainable improved yields). Obviously the second is a desirable policy objective. But to induce intensification in the low-density case would be premature because the factor ratios (principally labor to land) are not yet appropriate for intensification, population growth being much further behind.

Sustainable resource management and stable or even slowly improving economic yields may not assure stable or improving incomes. This consideration has led many observers to question whether the smallholder intensification that was adequate in the past can respond to recently accelerated rates of growth, and if not, whether a farming system will not relapse into a degradational mode (see, e.g., Lele and Stone, 1989). This view rests on the assumption that smallholder households are and must continue to be self-sufficient in food production, an assumption that underlies the concept of human carrying or supporting capacities. At the national level, such an assumption may be a policy directive.

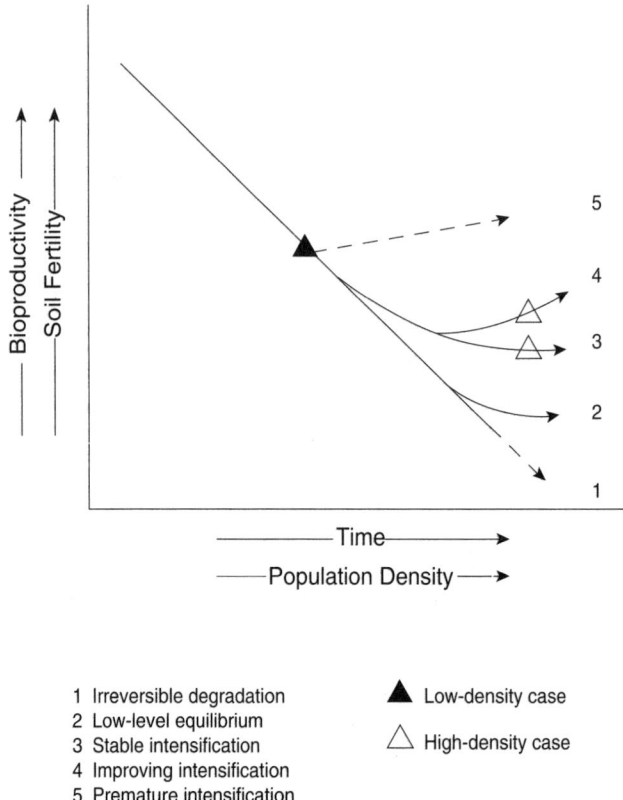

FIGURE 3 The transition from degradation to intensification in a farming system.

The assumption of self-sufficiency is not appropriate at the level of the farming system, at which the link between the population and the land is not immutable. In particular, the myth of a full-time farming peasantry, exclusively dependent on the produce of the smallholding, should be discarded. Migration and circulation reduce the demand for food and generate income. Food crops may be sold as well as market ("cash") crops. Agricultural incomes may be used to finance education or employment while off-farm earnings may be invested in agriculture or land improvement.[13]

---

[13] There are interesting parallels between the experience in the Kano farming system and in the Machakos District, Kenya, where rapid population growth has accompanied a transition from extensive to intensive farming and very substantial investments in land and water conservation during the last three decades (the preliminary output from this study is available in a series of working papers published by the Overseas Development Institute, London).

Wolman and Fournier's (1987:42) recommendation that "incentives need to be created for the farmers to remain on the land and make it produce" can be restated: "incentives should be created for smallholders to invest in the land to make it produce"—for even in the semiarid zone, the technical possibilities for increasing productivity have not been exhausted. But the risks to equity of unimpeded capitalization in land are considerable. Unless rights of access to land can be guaranteed (as was attempted in Kenya by land adjudication), the free operation of the market will have a negative effect. The new large landowners in northern Nigeria are not generally remarkable for their interest in intensification, conservation, or sustainability.

ACKNOWLEDGMENTS

The work reported in this paper was partly done under contract to the Federal Agricultural Co-Ordinating Unit, Ibadan, Nigeria, under the terms of the World Bank's Agricultural Sector loan to Nigeria, and the permission of the head of unit to publish it is gratefully acknowledged.

REFERENCES

Boserup, E.
    1965   *The Conditions of Agricultural Growth*. London: Allen and Unwin.

Bradley, A.K., S.B.J. MacFarlane, J.B. Moody, H.M. Gilles, J.G.C. Blacker, and B.D. Musa
    1982   Malumfashi Endemic Diseases Research Project XIX: demographic findings: population structure and fertility. *Annals of Tropical Medicine and Parasitology* 76:381-391.

Cline-Cole, R.A., J.A. Falola, H.A.C. Main, M.J. Mortimore, J.E. Nichol, and F.D. O'Reilly
    1990   *Woodfuel in Kano*. Tokyo: United Nations University Press.

Federal Department of Forestry
    1977   [Nigeria] Vegetation and Land Use, Map on the Scale 1:250,000. Ibadan, Nigeria: Federal Department of Forestry.

Field, N.J., and W.G. Collins
    1986   Land use from aerial photographs in the Nigerian savanna. Pp. 435-440 in M.C.J. Damen, G. Sicco Smit, and H. Th. Verstappen, eds., *Remote Sensing for Resources Development and Environmental Management*. Proceedings of the Seventh International Symposium, Enschede, 25-29 August. Rotterdam: Balkema.

Green, L.
    1970   *Population Models for National Planning*. Ibadan: Nigerian Institute for Social and Economic Research.

Grove, A.T.
    1961   Population densities and agriculture in Northern Nigeria. Pp. 115-136 in K.M. Barbour and R.M. Prothero, eds., *Essays on African Population*. London: Routledge and Kegan Paul.

Hill, J.
    1986   Kano ADP Fertilizer Study Results. Draft manuscript. Kano State Agricultural and Rural Development Authority, Kano, Nigeria.

Hill, P.
  1977 *Population, Prosperity and Poverty: Rural Kano, 1900 and 1970.* Cambridge, England: Cambridge University Press.
Jones, M.J., and A. Wild
  1975 *Soils of the West African Savanna: The Maintenance and Improvement of Their Fertility.* Harpenden, England: Commonwealth Agricultural Bureau.
Labaran, A.
  1987 Land appropriation for capitalized farming in the Sokoto region: some preliminary findings. Pp. 46-57 in M. Mortimore, E.A. Olofin, R.A. Cline-Cole, and A. Abdulkadir, eds., *Perspectives on Land Administration and Development in Nigeria.* Kano, Nigeria: Department of Geography, Bayero University.
Larson, W.E., and F.J. Pierce
  1991 Conservation and Enhancement of Soil Quality. Paper presented at the International Workshop for Evaluation for Sustainable Land Management in the Developing World, Chiang Rai, Thailand.
Lele, U., and S. Stone
  1989 Population Pressure, the Environment and Agricultural Intensification. Variations on the Boserup Hypothesis. *Madia Discussion Paper 4.* Washington, D.C.: World Bank.
Land Resources Development Centre
  1979 The Land Resources of Central Nigeria. *Land Resource Study 29.* Tolworth: Land Resources Development Centre, Overseas Development Administration.
McTainsh, G., and S. Stokes
  1980 Environmental Data Bank for Central Northern Nigeria. Users Guide. Kano, Nigeria: Department of Geography, Bayero University.
Mortimore, M.
  1967 Land and population pressure in the Kano Close-Settled Zone, Northern Nigeria. *The Advancement of Science* 23:677-688.
  1974 The demographic variable in regional planning in Kano State, Nigeria. Pp. 129-146 in B.S. Hoyle, ed., *Spatial Aspects of Development.* Chichester, England: John Wiley.
  1989a *Adapting to Drought. Farmers, Famines and Desertification in West Africa.* Cambridge, England: Cambridge University Press.
  1989b The Causes, Nature and Rate of Soil Degradation in the Northernmost States of Nigeria and an Assessment of the Role of Fertilizer in Counteracting the Processes of Degradation. Environment Department Working Paper 17. World Bank, Washington, D.C.
  1993 The intensification of peri-urban agriculture: the Kano Close-Settled Zone, 1964-86. In B.L. Turner, Jr., R.W. Kates, and G. Hyden, eds., *Population Growth and Agricultural Change in Africa.* Gainesville: University Press of Florida.
Mortimore, M.J., and J. Wilson
  1965 Land and people in the Kano Close-Settled Zone. Occasional Paper 1. Department of Geography, Ahmadu Bello University, Zaria, Nigeria.
Mortimore, M., E.U. Essiet, and S. Patrick
  1990 The Nature, Rate and Effective Limits of Intensification in the Smallholder Farming System of the Kano Close-Settled Zone. Report to the Federal Agricultural Coordinating Unit, Ibadan, Nigeria.
Morah, B.C., and O. Afolabi
  1984 Nigeria Fertility Survey, 1981/82. State Level Report: Kano State. National Population Bureau and World Fertility Survey, Lagos.

Pingali, P.L., Y. Bigot, and H.P. Binswanger
    1987   *Agricultural Mechanization and the Evolution of Farming Systems in Sub-Saharan Africa.* Baltimore: Johns Hopkins University Press.
Prothero, R.M.
    1958   Northern Nigeria Density of Population by Districts, 1952 Census. Federal Survey Department, Lagos.
    1962   Some observations on desiccation in North-Western Nigeria. *Erdkunde* 16:111-119.
Pullan, R.A.
    1974   Farmed parkland in West Africa. *Savanna* 3/2:119-152.
Turner, B.
    1977   The Fadama Lands of Central Northern Nigeria: Their Classification, Spatial Variation, Present and Potential Use. Unpublished Ph.D. dissertation, University of London.
Watts, M., ed.
    1987   *State, Oil and Agriculture in Nigeria.* Berkeley: Institute of International Studies, University of California.
Wolman, M.G., and F.G.A. Fournier, eds.
    1987   *Land Transformation in Agriculture.* Scientific Committee on Problems of the Environment 32. Chichester, England: John Wiley.
World Bank
    1984   *Population Change and Economic Development.* Washington, D.C.: World Bank.
Young, A.
    1993   Soil monitoring: a basic task for soil survey organisations. *Soil Use and Management* 7:126-130.

6
India: Population Pressure, Technology, Infrastructure, Capital Formation, and Rural Incomes

Robert E. Evenson

The real income consequences of population growth have long been a matter of policy concern. Malthus and Ricardo provided the classical analysis, showing that as populations grow relative to resources (including land, public infrastructure, and private and publicly held reproducible capital), downward pressure on labor incomes will result. A similar upward pressure on land rents would also take place. Because population growth increases with income, any set of conditions that produced an increase in real incomes would be followed by a rise in population growth, setting in motion forces bringing real labor incomes and population growth back to a subsistence equilibrium.[1]

This "dismal" prediction has been much modified in modern analysis. Modern analysts recognize that while a rise in incomes will lead to an increase in population growth, the associated rise in the price of (labor) time will generally induce a decrease in family size and population growth. This is because the "costs" of producing relatively "time-intensive" goods, such as children, typically rise more rapidly than does income. In addition, the income effect on child quality may dominate the income effect on child quantity, and this will also induce smaller family sizes.[2] Thus, escape from the Malthusian "trap" is possible.

---

[1] See Becker (1988) for a recent appraisal of these models.
[2] See Evenson (1991) for a review of the role of technology in agriculture.

Four investment activities are today deemed to be critical to generating the rising real income necessary to escape from the Malthusian trap. These are investments in: (1) public sector infrastructure, (2) publicly and privately held reproducible capital, (3) human capital, and (4) research to produce improved technology. There is ample historical evidence that these investments produce growth. Every modern developed economy can account for most of its real per capita economic growth in terms of these activities.[3]

A controversy remains, however, as to the effect of population growth in the presence of these activities. This is because it is alleged (a) that population growth itself induces some of the investments in growth-producing activities (Boserup), and (b) that large populations may actively enhance the effectiveness of some of the growth-producing activities via special types of scale economics (Verdoorn, Simon).[4] The modern literature on the "economic consequences of birth aversion" thus remains somewhat inconclusive as to whether these inducement and enhancement effects are sufficient to outweigh the fundamental classical, or Malthusian, effects.[5]

The real income consequences of improved technology are also subject to some debate. There is little doubt that technology, which enables more output per unit of input, increases aggregate income. However, because technology, especially agricultural technology, has a regional, or location-specific, dimension, the actual realization of these income gains between producers, consumers, and factors (i.e., labor, land) in different locations is unclear. It is quite possible that the introduction of improved technology will bring about economic losses for some groups.[6]

Because infrastructure and capital formation also have a regional or locational dimension, the growth in income that they produce will also have a complex distributional outcome. Furthermore, because population growth (pressure) also has a regional and locational dimension and because it has possible investment inducement and enhancement effects, population growth will interact with these activities in its effects on real income.

This paper reports an attempt to measure some of the real income impacts of population pressure, infrastructure, capital formation, and new technology in India. The first section of the chapter develops the analytic framework. The second section develops an empirical specification for testing the implications of this model and reports estimates. The third section discusses

---

[3] See Denison (1962); Jorgenson et al., (1988); and Antle and Capalbo (1988) for reviews.

[4] Lee et al. (1988) provided a review; see also Boserup (1965), Simon (1977, 1981), and Verdoorn (1951).

[5] See, for example, National Research Council (1986).

[6] Lipton and Longhurst (1989), among others, have reviewed some of this evidence.

the policy relevance of the findings. Appendix A provides an analytic model of population and technology impacts on earnings.

ANALYTIC ISSUES

A Simple One-Region Model

Consider the simplest possible case, in which only one product is produced and consumed. The market for the product is depicted in Figure 1.

The supply curve S_0 is determined by profit maximizing behavior of farmers for a given level of human capital skills, infrastructure, and technology. The curve shows how supply changes as prices change. An increase in technology, human capital, or infrastructure will shift the supply curve to the right, i.e., from S_0 to S_1. An increase in the number of laborers will also cause a rightward shift in the supply of the product because wages will fall. This, in turn, reduces the marginal cost and producers will produce a given quantity of output at a lower price.

The demand curve is derived from the utility-maximizing behavior of consumers for given tastes and for a given population. A shift (i.e., an increase) in population will shift the demand curve to the right. Figure 1 illustrates an important point regarding the impact of a technology-induced shift in the supply curve. The shift from S_0 to S_1 results in a fall in the equilibrium price from P_0 to P_1 and an increase in output from Y_0 to Y_1. The decline in price results in gains to consumers (measured by the area

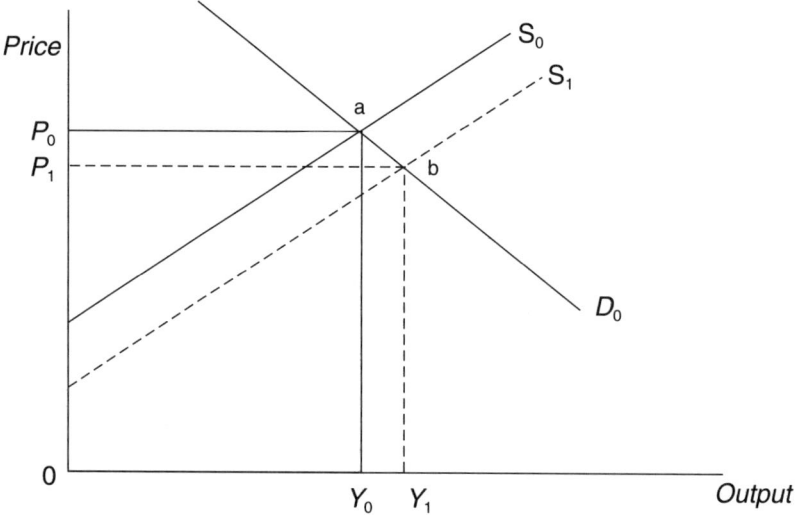

FIGURE 1 One-region model. D = demand, P = equilibrium price, S = supply, and Y = output.

$P_0 ab P_1$), and this decline is larger the more "inelastic" (with respect to price) is demand.

Revenue to the producer will change from the area $P_0 \cdot Y_0$ ($0 P_0 a Y_0$) to the area $P_1 \cdot Y_1$ ($0 P_1 b Y_1$), and this will be distributed between labor (N) and capital (K) according to the supply conditions for these factors (see below). Note that if demand is elastic with respect to price, that is, $\eta = (dY/dP)(P/Y)$ is less than -1, revenue to producers will rise. If it is inelastic, revenue will fall.

Appendix A develops a mathematical model for this simple case. The features of the model are:

1. shifter variables for population, technology, labor supply and capital supply are incorporated into the model;
2. an equation showing how equilibrium prices of labor and capital are affected by these shifters is derived;
3. the analysis shows that the growth rate of the equilibrium wage rate, a key variable for income analysis because low-income families earn the bulk of their income from wages, is affected in the following ways by the shifters:

(a) An increase in technology (or infrastructure) has a positive impact on (nominal) wages if demand is elastic. This is because total revenues increase when demand is elastic, as they do when the good is internationally traded. When demand is inelastic the growth in nominal wages will be lower, but the growth in real wages when technology increases is generally positive because the price of the product falls.

(b) The effect on wages of an increase in the capital stock (i.e., a shift in the supply of capital) will depend on the ease with which capital can be substituted for labor. If it is relatively easy to substitute the more abundant capital for labor, nominal wages will be reduced. The effect also depends on the elasticity of demand. The more elastic is demand, the more likely it is that increased capital will aid labor.

(c) The effect of an increase in population can be considered in two parts. The size of the labor force increases along with the population. An increase in the number of workers has a negative effect on wages. Population growth, on the other hand, increases demand, and this has a positive effect on wages. The combined impact depends on the ease of substituting labor for capital and on the elasticity of demand. In an economy in which there is little or no capital (a classical Malthusian economy), the effect of population growth on wages is negative. If the economy is capitalized and labor can be easily substituted for capital, population growth can lead to higher nominal (and real) wages.

(d) When the capital stock grows at the same rate as the labor force and population, wages do not change.

An Extension to Two Regions

These results are derived under the supposition that all producers have equal access to technology. Many studies have shown that agricultural technology is quite location specific, so that technology suited to one region is not actually available for another.

It is simple to extend Figure 1 to a two-region case to obtain a basic insight about regionalization (see Figure 2).

Because suppliers are competitive, the supply curves can be added up for any price. Suppose in the two regions, 1 and 2, S_{10} is the supply curve for region 1 producers. The total supply curve for both regions is $S_{10} + S_{20}$. The initial market equilibrium is at P_0, with Y_{10} produced in region 1 and Y_{20} in region 2.

Now suppose technical change shifts the supply function for region 2, but not region 1. Most new agricultural technology is location specific and some regions are advantaged, others disadvantaged. The equilibrium price falls to P_1, and region 1 producers now produce less ($Y_{10} - Y_{11}$). Region 2 producers will produce more $Y_{21} - Y_{20}$ and they produce more under all demand conditions.

Thus it is clear that producers in region 1 will lose revenue as a result of technology introduced in region 2 unless demand is perfectly elastic. Returns to fixed factors in region 1 will decline (by $P_0 a c P_1$) if labor is perfectly mobile, that is, if it moves freely from one region to another. It is,

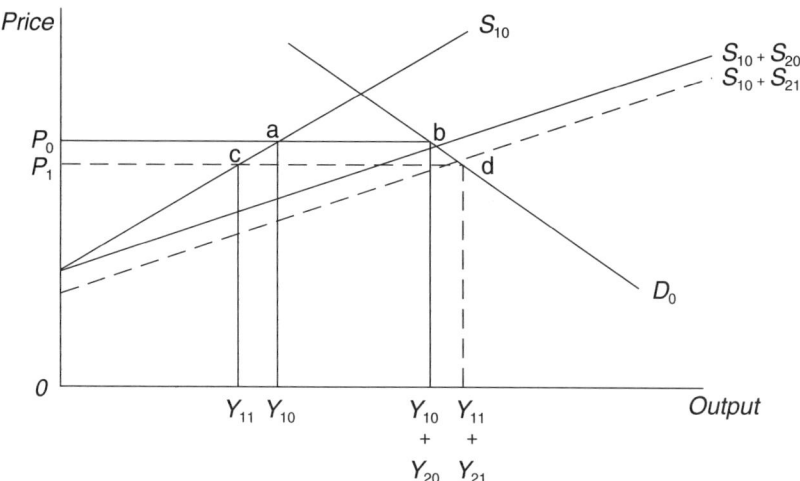

FIGURE 2 Two-region model. D = demand, P = price, S = supply, and Y = output.

of course, possible that labor markets may be segmented, i.e., that labor will not move easily from region 1 to 2.

One can intuitively see that if labor is not mobile, region 1 will suffer a wage decline (and this will affect S_{10}, shifting it rightward, partially restoring the production and employment effect). Returns to fixed factors will also fall in region 1, but not as much as they would if the labor markets were not segmented. Conversely, in region 2 a segmented labor market will permit a wage rise, shifting S_{21} upward and modifying the gains to fixed factors as well as to output and employment.

However, if labor is mobile, wages will be the same in both regions. Wages will thus fall less in region 1 and rise less in region 2 than they would in a segmented market (the actual change will be governed by the [η + 1] condition [see equation 10 in Appendix A]). This will accentuate the loss to fixed factors in region 1 and the gain to fixed factors in region 2.

It is important to note that in a segmented labor market, labor in the disadvantaged region will be harmed by technological gains in the advantaged region as long as demand is not perfectly elastic. However, when labor is mobile it may gain from technical change in the advantaged region as long as demand is elastic. Labor in the advantaged region will gain from its own technology as long as its demand is elastic. This gain will depend on the mobility of labor.

This same logic applies to differential population growth in a region. Slower population and labor force growth have the same effect as more rapid technology growth.

An Extension to Three Regions

The two-region model can be easily extended to a three-region model. Figure 3 depicts such a model. It shows a supply shift in region 2. This shift with no labor mobility will reduce the demand for labor in regions 1 and 3 and increase demand in region 2. With mobility, labor will move from (1) to (2) and from (3) to (2), shifting the technology effect to land or fixed-factor rents.

This three-region perspective is useful in terms of analyzing limited mobility as well. Suppose that labor moves easily from (1) to (2) but not from (1) to (3). Then technical change in (2) could have a positive impact on wages in (1) whereas technical change in (3) would have a negative effect on wages in (1). Accordingly, distance and other barriers to migration are important factors to consider in assessing technical change and population effects for advantaged and disadvantaged regions.

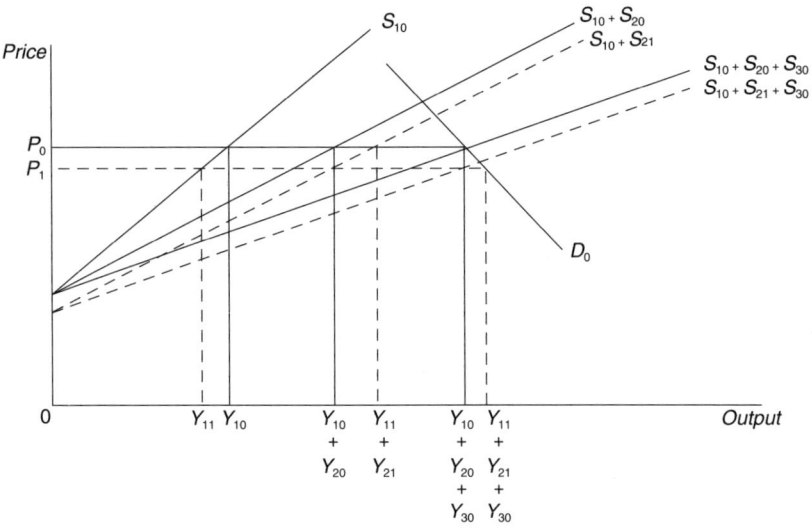

FIGURE 3 Three-region model. D = demand, P = price, S = supply, and Y = output.

EMPIRICAL TESTS: AN APPLICATION TO INDIA

Two empirical strategies for testing the impact of population growth on real income are available. The first is the construction of a "general equilibrium" model in which product markets and factor markets are modeled from econometrically estimated supply and demand functions. Population, technology, and infrastructure variables can then be included in these equation estimates. Given a properly estimated model, simulations can be carried out in which population, technology, and infrastructure change impacts on equilibrium prices and quantities can be estimated (or simulated). From these estimated changes in prices and quantities, real-income effects on particular groups (e.g., landless households or small farmers) can be simulated (see Evenson, 1991).

The second strategy is to estimate a "reduced-form" specification of determinants of real wages and rental income in agriculture. Technology, population, and infrastructure variables can be included in this analysis. This strategy is somewhat more amenable to estimating enhancement and inducement effects of population pressure and it also enables much simpler measurement of regional technology effects. The second strategy is pursued here for rural India for the 1959-1984 period.

The strategy used in this study is undertaken in two stages. In the first stage an induced investment analysis is undertaken in which lagged population density variables are treated as predictors of investment in agricultural research, agricultural extension, rural roads, rural markets, and changes in net irrigated area and net cropped areas. This analysis shows that while a considerable amount of investment could be treated as being induced by population change, much of this investment was the result of strategic planning. Accordingly, it was not deemed appropriate to predict investment from the Stage I equation for use in the second stage, but rather to utilize these estimates as auxiliary estimates of induced effects.

The second stage then entailed an analysis of real returns to labor and to land for farmers and laborers in India. The determining variables were population growth, technology flows—both domestically produced and imported—and infrastructure. These variables were specified as "stock" variables (in contrast to the investment variables in Stage I). Population density variables are interacted with these variables to estimate population enhancement effects.

Variable Definitions and Means—Stage I

Table 1 summarizes the Stage I variables.[7] The dependent variables are annual investment in research and extension (technology), rural markets and roads (infrastructure), irrigation, and new cropped area. Each of these variables is treated as jointly determined by the full set of exogenous determining variables.

The determining variables are lagged stock variables. The population density, or "pressure," variable is computed as the 1956 state rural population divided by the 1984 net cropped area. Note that this is not a population growth variable. The 1984 net cropped area is treated as a better measure of potential cultivable land than is the 1956 level of net cropped area. This variable is computed for the state rather than the district to achieve more "exogeneity." (The dependent variables are district-level variables, although for research and extension these are effectively state-level variables.) The actual estimates included a number of interaction variables (discussed below).

Variable Definitions and Means—Stage II

Table 2 reports similar variable definitions for the second-stage analysis. The endogenous dependent variables are the index of real wages paid to rural workers and the index of estimated market rents for land. Note that both are measured at the district level and all are indexed on 1956-1959

---

[7]See Evenson and McKinsey (1991) for a full description of the data.

TABLE 1 Variable Definitions and Means: Stage I Analysis

Variable	Definition	Mean	SD
I. Endogenous (dependent)			
RESEXP	Annual real expenditures on research in the state	252	324
EXT	Annual man-days of extension per district	3.79	3.93
IMKTS	Number of markets in the district, indexed to 1956 = 1	2.30	2.62
INROADL	Road length per net cropped area in 1984 in district, indexed to 1956 = 1	1.744	1.927
INIA	Net irrigated area in district, indexed to 1956 = 1	2.160	2.296
INCA	Net cropped area in district, indexed to 1956 = 1	1.064	0.142
II. Exogenous (independent)			
MSPDEN	State population in 1956 net cropped area in 1984	3006	1843
LITERACY	Percentage of rural males who are literate	0.307	0.104
IADP	Dummy = 1 for intensive agriculture district	0.035	0.182
MNCA	State mean net cropped area per district (000 ha)	477	272
MNIA	State mean net irrigated area per district (000 ha)	70	77
WHYV	Percentage of cereals planted in high-yielding varieties	0.124	0.183
ISOUT-IN	Index of state total factor productivity gains (1956 = 1)	1.22	0.27
INOUT-IN	Index of geoclimatic neighbor total factor productivity gains (1956 = 1)	1.25	0.23
IFOUT - IN	Index of other district total factor productivity gains	1.27	0.22
AGRO	Agroclimatic region dummies	—	
YEAR	Time (1956-1987)	—	
YEAR^2	YEAR squared	—	

values. Thus in the reduced form model underlying these variables, the 1956-1959 differences between districts are treated as predetermined by a number of social and economic factors (including population density) prior to the postindependence period. Changes in these returns to labor and land over the 1956-1959 to 1983-1984 period are thus the object of analysis.

The determining variables are population, technology, and infrastructure variables. Population is modeled as having an "enhancement" effect and a growth effect. Two population variables are constructed, both at the state level (to avoid endogeneity as much as possible). The MSPDEN variable is a population pressure variable and it is treated as the enhancing variable (in interaction with other variables). The ISPDEN variable is a growth variable indexed as being equal to one during 1956-1959 at the state level. Thus, population growth is treated as exogenous to the district on the grounds that it is determined primarily by other dependent variables in the analysis as well as by the natural process of population growth. It is treated as an inducing variable.

TABLE 2 Variable Definitions and Means: Stage II Analysis

Variable	Definition	Means All India	N. India
I. Endogenous (dependent)			
IRWAGE	Rural wages paid to male laborers, deflated by worker CPI, indexed to 1956 = 1	1.017	1.100
IPNCA	Reported land rent per ha Net cropped area deflated by CPI, indexed to 1956 = 1	2.614	2.372
II. Exogenous (independent)			
ISPDEN	State rural population/net cropped area in 1984, indexed to 1956 = 1	1.254	1.252
MSPDEN	State population in 1956, net cropped area in 1984	3024	3301
NIAI	District ratio of net irrigated area/net cropped area	0.238	0.435
MKTS	Rural markets per district	10.66	12.37
LITERACY	Percentage of rural males literate	0.308	0.294
ROADL	District road length/net cropped area 1984	2001	1186
IADP	Dummy = for 1 intensive agricultural district	0.035	0.031
WHYV	Percentage of cereal acreage planted in high-yielding varieties	0.126	0.154
IOUT-IN	District total factor productivity, indexed to 1956-1959 = 1	1.217	1.339
ISOUT-IN	State of total factor productivity index, 1956-1959 = 1	1.212	1.341
INOUT-IN	Geoclimatic neighbor district total factor productivity index, 1956-1959 = 1	1.247	1.341
IFOUT-IN	Nonneighbor district total factor productivity index, 1956-59 = 1	1.276	1.194
YEAR			

The technology variables are of two types. The WHYV, which measures the proportion of area planted in high-yielding varieties, is treated as measuring one component of new technology, much of it imported from abroad. This variable is endogenous at the farm level but can be considered to be exogenous at the district level.[8]

---

[8]This is because geoclimatic factors dominate the adoption of high-yielding varieties at the district level.

The main technology variables, however, are the Divisia-based total factor productivity (TFP) indexes. These are defined for the district, for the state in which the district is located, for the districts outside the state but in the same geoclimatic region, and for all other districts. The attempt here is to measure the differential impact of technology in the district and in other regions (as discussed in Figure 3).[9] Other variables measure infrastructure and capital stock variables.

Stage I Estimates

Table 3 summarizes the Stage I estimates of population-induced investment effects. The regression estimates utilized a common set of independent variables including several "interaction" variables. The impacts shown in Table 3 are "elasticities" computed at sample means. Table B-1 in Appendix B reports the full regression estimates.

The major variable of interest is the population pressure variable, MSPDEN. These estimates show that population pressure induces significant investment in agricultural research (but not enough to offset population growth, i.e., the elasticity is less than one). Population pressure also induces some investment in agricultural extension. The interaction of the population pressure variable with the HYV (high-yielding varieties) access variable strengthens these technology inducement effects.

Population pressure has mixed impacts on infrastructure. It appears to stimulate road investments but does not stimulate the development of improved rural markets. The road-inducement effect is strengthened by HYV availability (some of these HYVs were imported from abroad).

The effect of population density on irrigation and cropped areas is negligible. The level of adult literacy appears to have relatively minor impacts on investments, except for small extension and irrigation impacts.

Past technological changes have some regional effects, but on the whole the net overall effect of past technological success on investment is minor. HYV availability does not induce significant investments. The IADP (intensive agricultural district) effects are minor (though not in the IADP districts, where they did have major impacts on markets, roads, and irrigation).

Research investment tends to respond positively to the state's own productivity record, but negatively to the production change in competing regions. This is also the case for extension investment. It appears that states do not attempt to invest to facilitate spill-in technology from outside the state except in markets and irrigation. (The geoclimatic neighbors variable

---

[9]Geoclimatic regions are discussed in Evenson and McKinsey (1991).

TABLE 3 Stage I Estimates: Population- and Technology-Induced Investment Elasticities

Determining Variable	Research (RESEXP)	Extension (EXT)	Markets (IMKTS)	Roads (IROADL)	Irrigation (INIA)	Cropped Area (INCA)
MSPDEN	.757	.151	-.183	.517	-.002	-.067
LITERACY	-.136	.114	.082	-.119	.251	-.031
MNCA	-.092	-.138	.159	.310	.154	-.058
MNIA	.055	.109	.009	-.068	-.324	-.009
WHYV	-.111	-.111	.066	-.027	-.017	-.027
IADP	-.002	-.002	.025	.012	.009	.001
ISOUT-IN	.938	.731	-.195	.047	-.291	-.027
INOUT-IN	.078	-.649	.223	-.478	.135	.042
IFOUT-IN	-.973	-.603	-.103	.357	.388	.074
R^2	.642	.833	.289	.323	.299	.264
F	422	1,175	95	112	100	84

[INOUT-IN] represents the potential spill-in technology.) If all regions realize productivity gains at the same rate, the net effects of past productivity history are very small.

Proponents of the "invisible institutional hand" by which public sector investments are made in some optimizing fashion will be disappointed by these estimates. The determining variables explain only a relatively small part of actual investment. Investment in research and extension increased more rapidly than did population growth, for example.[10]

It is reasonable, however, to recognize that effective public investment is a proactive process entailing analysis, judgment, and political considerations. It is not a simple reactive process in which population density truly induces a substantial amount of investment. (Note, however, that this analysis did not include a population growth variable—see the next section. Accordingly, it would be improper to attempt to predict the "stocks" used in the Stage II analysis from these investment equations.)

Stage II Reduced Form, Income Determinant Estimates

The Stage II income determinant estimates are summarized in Table 4. As with Table 3, these estimates are reported as computed elasticities. Population enhancement interactions are noted. (Table B-2 in Appendix B reports actual estimates.)

Estimates are reported for all India (i.e., 10 states), and for four North India states. North India has benefited most from new HYV and other technology, and it is generally regarded to be the more progressive and development-oriented region of India (although it includes many poor districts).

The dependent variables are the real wages for rural (generally landless) daily workers (including payments in kind), indexed on 1956 = 1 in each district, and the real rental rate for land, which is also indexed on 1956 = 1. Thus, this is an analysis of changes in real labor and land incomes over the 1956-1984 period. The determining variables include two population variables, five infrastructure variables, and five technology variables.

The population variables are the density variable, MSPDEN, used in Stage I to measure induced investment effects, and IMSPDN, a growth index of rural laborers for the state. The population density variable is interacted with infrastructure and technology variables to measure enhancement effects. The growth variable measures the direct impact of population on incomes. (This could have been interacted as well but the basic notion

---

[10]Hayami and Ruttan (1971), for example, suggest that public system response to economic opportunities is high.

of enhancement is a density notion.) The growth variable is treated as exogenously determined by general population growth. Migration between states is viewed as being determined by other dependent variables including the initial density.

Two sets of elasticities are reported. The first (1) is computed from the second stage estimates. The second (2) adds the population-induced effects from the first stage estimates to these.[11]

Real Labor Income Effects

Consider the population effects. The labor force growth variable shows a clear negative impact on real wage incomes in all India and in North India. This is a large and significant effect (–.276 and –.333). The density enhancement effects are positive for all India and for North India (.026 and .096). The computed density-inducement effects are also positive (.112 and .033), and the combined enhancement and inducement effects (which interact positively with technology) are also significant. They do not outweigh the negative growth effects of population, however. For all India, the positive enhancement and inducement effects are half of the negative growth effect. For North India they are approximately 40 percent of the negative growth effects. This estimate is approximately the same as an earlier estimate for North India computed from a general equilibrium model for an earlier period (Evenson, 1991).

Although the population impacts on real labor incomes are roughly the same for North India and all India, the relative impacts of infrastructure and technology differ. For all India, both infrastructure and technology contribute to higher labor incomes, although technology is more important. For North India, infrastructure contributions are negligible and technology contributions are large. (These technology impacts are enhanced by population density in North India but not in all India.)

For all India the infrastructure impact of roads and labor income is important. Interestingly, irrigation impacts are relatively low. Literacy also has a small impact, as do markets. For North India these impacts are overwhelmed by technology impacts.

The technology impacts require interpretation in the context of the advantaged-disadvantaged region model (Figure 3). Availability of high-yielding varieties has a large positive impact on labor incomes in regions where it occurs.

---

[11] These calculations are based on productivity weights. That is, population growth induces more research, this in turn produces more total factor productivity, which in turn affects wages (rents). The research total factor productivity elasticities as well as the effects of markets, roads, etc., on total factor productuvity are taken from Evenson and McKinsey (1991).

TABLE 4 Stage II Estimates: Population, Technology, and Infrastructure Impacts on Real Rural Wages and Land Rents

	Real Wages					
	Population Enhancement Effects		Elasticity (1)		Elasticity (2)	
Determining Variable	All India	North India	All India	North India	All India	North India
Population						
Growth (IMSPDN)			−0.276	−0.333		
Density (MSPDEN)			0.026	0.096	0.138	0.129
Infrastructure						
Markets (MKTS)	−	−	0.016	0.068	0.013	−0.052
Roads (ROADL)	−	+	0.195	0.001	0.295	0.001
Irrigation (NIA1)	+	−	0.045	−0.013	0.048	−0.014
Literacy	+	−	0.026	−0.013		
Intensive agricultural district	+	−	−0.002	−0.002		
Technology						
High-yielding varieties (WHYV)	+	+	0.003	0.077		
District total factor productivity	−	+	−0.014	0.189		
State total factor productivity	−	−	−0.022	−0.398		
Neighbor total factor productivity	+	+	0.441	0.927		
Nonneighbor total factor productivity	−	−	0.151	−0.175		
Total			0.257	0.620	0.254	0.672

NOTE: Elasticity (1) includes enhancement effects only. Elasticity (2) includes enhancement plus inducement effects.

For all India the regional estimates indicate that the productivity gains realized outside the state but in neighboring (in a geoclimatic sense) districts increase real labor incomes. District and state productivity gains have little effect. Productivity gains from "far neighbors" are competitive and reduce labor incomes. This suggests that labor mobility is important and that it has been sufficient to create a large region in which productivity gains can benefit laborers. Labor mobility, however, is not sufficient to eliminate the competitive effect from far neighbors. Note further that popu-

Land Prices					
Population Enhancement Effects		Elasticity (1)		Elasticity (2)	
All India	North India	All India	North India	All India	North India
		−0.530	0.843		
		−1.212	−0.292	−1.264	−0.342
−	−	0.051	0.017	0.042	0.014
+	+	0.051	0.017	0.042	0.014
−	−	−0.1048	−0.072	−0.045	−0.077
+	+	0.028	0.152		
−	−	0.003	−0.095		
−	−	0.080	−0.221		
+	−	−0.406	−0.035		
−	−	0.173	−0.289		
+	+	−0.820	−0.230		
		−0.970	−0.870	−1.02	−0.909

lation density enhances the ability of workers to gain from the productivity of nearby neighbors, i.e., by enlarging the region for mobility. Note also that population density worsens the competitive impact from far neighbors. If all regions realize the same rate of total factor productivity gains, the total effect of improved technology on labor incomes would be positive and significant. (Indeed a 1 percent total factor productivity gain more than offsets the net loss from a 1 percent growth in population.)

For North India, where technology in the form of green revolution wheat (and rice) varieties has been more important, technology impacts are larger. The regional implications are slightly different. The nearby neighbor and far neighbor effects are similar to those for all India. The state and district estimates suggest a kind of submarket for labor. There appears to be a local effect (possibly a short-term effect for the abruptness of the green revolution) in which laborers gain from local technology (in addition to high-yielding variety technology and lose as a result of competition from other districts in the state. There is enough of an enhancement of mobility due to population to enable workers to benefit from near neighbors' productivity gains.

Land Income Effects

The estimated land income effects are generally consistent with the labor income estimates, with prior studies, and with economic logic. This is true despite very crude land price data.

For all India, the population impacts are negative on land incomes. For North India the growth impact is positive, whereas the enhancement and inducement impacts are negative. The enhancement and inducement effects are consistent with the negative effects of technology because these activities create substitutes for land and make it less scarce. Irrigation does as well. Markets and literacy appear to have complementary effects.

The differences in the population growth impact on land incomes between all India and North India may be due to differences in land scarcity and possibly to off-farm income opportunities. If land is scarce, population growth should have the Malthusian effect measured in North India.

SUMMARY

The reduced form estimates of the effects of population, infrastructure, and technology on labor and land incomes in India are consistent with theoretical expectations and with prior evidence from North India.

For population effects these estimates show that the Malthusian labor supply has negative impacts on labor incomes and that the impacts are partially but not fully offset by population inducement and enhancement effects. The direct growth effects on land incomes differ for North India and all India, but population enhancement and inducement effects are negative on land incomes. Infrastructure effects are small, although the existence of roads is important to labor income. Irrigation has only small effects.

New technology raises labor incomes and lowers land incomes, and these effects are stronger in North India. The geographic size of the labor market impacts due to regional productivity change is large, but does not cover the entire country. There is a competitive regional impact where advantaged regional productivity growth reduces both labor (and land) incomes in disadvantaged regions (that is, regions not receiving the technology). Population density enlarges the area of the region that gains.

From a distributional perspective, these results support policy interventions to slow population growth (actually labor force growth) and international migration in all regions. More infrastructure investment is also called for.

Perhaps of most relevance is the very strong implication for technology. Improved technology raises rural labor income unless it is very unevenly produced, in which case productivity gains in advantaged regions may reduce labor incomes in disadvantaged regions. However, existing mobility appears to be sufficient to enable locally disadvantaged regions to escape this reduction, indeed to gain from nearby advantaged neighbors. On balance, improved technology is a major factor enabling rural India to escape, at least temporarily, the Malthusian population trap.

REFERENCES

Antle, S.M., and J.M. Capalbo, eds.
    1988   *Agricultural Productivity: Measurement and Explanation.* Washington, D.C.: Resources for the Future.

Becker, G.S.
    1988   Family economics and macro behavior. *The American Economic Review* 78:1-13.

Boserup, E.
    1965   *The Conditions of Agricultural Growth.* Chicago: Aldine.

Denison, E.
    1962   *The Sources of Economic Growth in the United States and the Alternatives Before Us.* New York: Committee for Economic Development.

Evenson, R.E.
    1979   Technology access and factor markets in agriculture. *Philippine Economic Journal.* 1&2:1-16.
    1991   Technology, infrastructure, output supply and factor demand in North Indian agriculture. Pp. 217-232 in R.E. Evenson and C.E. Pray, eds., *Research and Productivity in Asian Agriculture.* Ithaca, N.Y.: Cornell University Press.

Evenson, R.E., and J. McKinsey
    1991   Research, extension, infrastructure, and productivity change in Indian agriculture. Pp. 158-184 in R.E. Evenson and C.E. Pray, eds., *Research and Productivity in Asian Agriculture.* Ithaca, N.Y.: Cornell University Press.

Hayami, Y., and V. Ruttan
    1971   *Agricultural Development: An International Perspective.* Baltimore: Johns Hopkins University Press.

Jorgenson, D., F. Gollop, and B. Fraumeni
    1988   *Productivity and U.S. Economic Growth.* Cambridge, Mass.: Harvard University Press.

Lee, R.D., W.B. Arthur, A.C. Kelley, G. Rogers, and T.N. Srinivasan, eds.
    1988   *Population, Food and Rural Development.* Oxford: Clarendon Press.

Lipton, M., and R. Longhurst
    1989   *New Seeds and Poor People.* Baltimore: Johns Hopkins University Press.

National Research Council
 1986 *Population Growth and Economic Development: Policy Questions.* Committee on Population. Washington, D.C.: National Academy Press.

Simon, J.
 1977 *The Economics of Population Growth.* Princeton, N.J.: Princeton University Press.
 1981 *The Ultimate Resource.* Princeton, N.J.: Princeton University Press.

Verdoorn, P.J.
 1951 On an empirical law governing the productivity of labor. *Econometrica* 19:209-210.

APPENDIX A:
AN ANALYTIC MODEL OF POPULATION AND TECHNOLOGY IMPACTS ON EARNINGS

A Simple, Single-Region Model

Consider a single product (Y_s) produced in a single region using labor (L) and an aggregate capital stock (K). The production function, F( ), can be written as:

$$Y_s = T(t)F(N,K), \quad T^* = dT(t)/dt, \tag{1}$$

where T(t) is a neutral technology index governing all producers of Y. A shift in technology will cause more output per unit of input and will not cause the cost minimizing mix of N and K to change.

The demand for the product (D(Y,I), depicted as D_0 in Figure 1) may be written as:

$$Y_d = P(t)D(Y,I), \quad P^* = dP(t)/dt, \tag{2}$$

where Y_d is quantity demanded and P(t) is a population index.

Now consider the supply functions for N and K, $g(P_N)$ and $k(P_K)$:

$$N = N(t)\, g(P_N), \; N^* = dN(t)/dt; \; \varepsilon_N = (dg/dP_N)(P_N/N) \tag{3}$$

and

$$K = K(t)\, k(P_K), \; K^* = dK(t)/dt; \; \varepsilon_k = (dK/dP_K)P_K/K). \tag{4}$$

In equation 3 the supply of labor responds to the wage rate P_N and to a shift variable, N^*, which may be considered to be population-related labor force growth. The supply of capital has a similar policy-related shifter.

Producers will maximize profits (π) for any set of output prices and input prices:

$$\Pi = P_Y Y - P_N N - P_K K. \tag{5}$$

Solving first-order conditions for Y, N, and K and substituting into equation 5 yields the *maximized profits* function:

$$\Pi^* = \pi(P_Y, P_N, P_K, T^*, P^*, N^*, K^*). \tag{6}$$

Note that this maximized profit function includes the four "shift factors," T* (technology), P* (population), N* (also population and migration), and K* (capital and infrastructure). These shift factors also belong in the product supply and factor demand equation derived from profit-maximizing behavior via Shephards' Lemma:

$$\partial \Pi* / \partial P_Y = Y_S = Y_S(P_Y, P_N, P_K, T^*, P^*, N^*, K^*), \tag{7}$$

$$\partial \Pi* / \partial P_N = N_D = N_D(P_Y, P_N, P_K, T^*, P^*, N^*, K^*), \tag{8}$$

$$\partial \Pi^* / \partial P_K = K_D = K_D(P_Y, P_N, P_K, T^*, P^*, N^*, K^*). \tag{9}$$

Technology and population growth also shift the demand for N and K (see equations 8 and 9.)

Expressions for these latter effects can be derived in this model by differentiating the system of equations 1-4 and equation 6 with respect to time and solving for the equilibrium growth rates in the price of factors. This yields:

$$\dot{P}_N / P_N = \frac{1}{\Delta}[(\sigma + \varepsilon_K)P^*/P - (\eta + 1)T^*/T - S_K(\sigma + \eta)K^*/K \\ -(S_N \sigma - S_K \eta + \varepsilon_K)N^*/N] \tag{10}$$

and

$$\dot{P}_K / P_K \frac{1}{\Delta} = [(\sigma + \varepsilon_N)P^*/P - (\eta + 1)T^*/T - S_N(\sigma + \eta)K^*/K \\ -(S_K \sigma - S_N \eta + \varepsilon_N)N^*/N] \tag{11}$$

These expressions relate the equilibrium price paths of labor and capital ($\dot{P}_N / P_N$ and $\dot{P}_K / P_K$ expressed as percentage rates of change) to changes in each of the shifter variables (P*/P, T*/T, K*/K, and N*/N, also expressed as rates of change). The additional parameters of the model are:

the factor supply elasticities, ε_N and ε_K;
the output demand elasticity, η;
the elasticity of substitution between N and K, σ;
the factor cost shares S_N and S_K; and
the term $\Delta = -\eta(\varepsilon_N \varepsilon_K + S_K \varepsilon_N) + \varepsilon_K \varepsilon_N + S_N \varepsilon_N + S_K \varepsilon_K - \eta \sigma$. Note that Δ is positive as each term in the expression is positive.

Equation 10 is particularly important for policy analysis. It provides the basic analysis of the impacts of population and technology on returns to labor. The impact of technical change T*/T, can be seen to depend on the elasticity of demand (as discussed in connection with Figure 1). If demand is elastic ([η + 1] is negative, hence –[η + 1] is positive), faster technical change will be associated with higher rates of change in the price of labor. These in turn will be higher the higher are σ and ε_K. The reverse will hold for inelastic demand. The effect of technical change on capital prices is similar. However, the distribution of gains (or losses) between labor and capital will depend on relative supply elasticities. The factor with the most inelastic supply will receive a relatively larger part of the gains. In fact, reference to Figure 1 will show that if K is strictly a fixed factor, its return will be the triangle P_0ac initially and will change to the triangle P_1bd after the new technology is introduced. These returns will not fall even when demand is inelastic.

The effect of an increase in capital, K^*/K, on labor depends on the term $(\sigma + \eta)$. If this is negative, expanding the capital stock will help labor. For example, a credit subsidy to capital will lead to a positive K^*/K. If it is easy to substitute this subsidized capital for labor, i.e., if σ is high, it is more likely that labor will be harmed by this policy. If the product is traded internationally, i.e., η is large and negative, it is more likely that labor (and capital) will be helped (by the subsidy).

Equation 10 can be rewritten as equation 12 to better analyze the effects of population, P^*/P, and labor force growth, N^*/N:

$$\dot{P}_N / P_N = \frac{1}{\Delta}[(\sigma + \varepsilon_K)(P^*/P - N^*/N) - (\eta+1)T^*/T \\ - S_K(\sigma + \eta)(K^*/K - N^*/N)] \tag{12}$$

The effect of labor force growth, N^*/N, on labor earnings is negative because the second term, which depends on $\sigma + \eta$, cannot become positive enough as η gets large and negative because η is in Δ.

The effect of population growth, P^*/P_1, is positive on labor earnings. The combined effect of population and labor force growth, $P^*/P = N^*/N$, is dependent only on the $\sigma + n$ term. If σ is high and η low, population growth can actually lead to rising wages. Of course, the classical economists had in mind $\sigma = 0$, so population growth had a negative impact on labor earnings. One can also see that if $K^*/K = N^*/N = P^*/P$, there will be no effect on $\dot{P}_N/P_N$.

It should further be noted that no inducement or enhancement effects have been considered so far. If P^*/P "induced" an expansion in K^*/K, this would be a positive offset in a classical world ($\sigma = 0$). If P^*/P enhanced T^*T, it could lead to a positive or negative effect.

An Extension to Two Regions

The expression for wage effects in region 1 when technology can occur in region 1 or 2 is the analogue to equation 10:

$$\dot{P}/P(1) = \frac{1}{\Delta}\left\{(\sigma+\varepsilon)\left[P*/P - \eta\left(\frac{1-m}{S_1}\right) - 1\right]\frac{T*_1}{S_1} + \left[\eta\left(\frac{1-m}{S_2}\right) - 1\right]\frac{T*_2}{T_2}\right. \\ \left. - S_K(\sigma+\eta)K*/K - S_K\sigma + S_K(\eta+\varepsilon_K)N*/N\right\} \quad (13)$$

when m is a mobility index for labor that ranges from 0 (no mobility) to 1 (perfect mobility).

APPENDIX B: DATA TABLES

TABLE B-1 Stage I Regression Estimates

Dependent Variable	RESEXP		EXT		IMKTS	
INTERCEPT	768413	(41.22)	73954	(47.38)	11708	
MSPDEN	0.0344	(6.14)	0.001	(14.59)	−0.000	
LITERACY	533.350	(3.20)	5.097	(3.69)	−5.957	
IADP	−16.181	(−1.11)	−0.202	(−1.67)	1.668	
MNCA	−0.042	(−3.29)	−0.001	(−8.83)	0.006	
MNIA	0.299	(5.87)	0.001	(11.17)	−0.000	
HYV	−1518.230	(−11.76)	−21.338	(−19.94)	4.192	
WHYVLIT	−877.629	(−4.52)	13.901	(8.65)	7.650	
LITPOP	−0.009	(−0.57)	−0.002	(−14.62)	0.001	
WHYVPOP	0.257	(22.51)	0.001	(9.48)	−0.001	
WHYVMNCA	−0.050	(0.71)	−0.002	(−2.59)	0.001	
WHYVMNIA	−0.820	(−4.96)	0.001	(6.75)	0.005	
HYVOUTIN	713.561	(10.89)	9.024	(16.63)	−3.637	
LITOUTIN	−417.363	(−3.34)	0.392	(0.38)	2.515	
ISOUT-IN	223.892	(5.43)	1.034	(3.03)	−0.690	
IMOUT-IN	15.897	(0.83)	−1.972	(−12.44)	0.417	
IFOUT-IN	−193.430	(−9.23)	−1.802	(−10.38)	−0.188	
AGRO2	−106.034	(−5.31)	−1.827	(−11.05)	1.303	
AGRO3	−60.185	(−3.76)	0.435	(3.28)	0.796	
AGRO4	−61.476	(−4.12)	−1.004	(−8.12)	0.334	
AGRO5	−125.205	(−6.12)	−0.768	(−4.53)	2.872	
AGRO6	−71.011	(−4.45)	−1.088	(−8.23)	1.567	
AGRO7	−103.801	(−5.33)	−1.181	(−11.23)	1.944	
YEAR	−7834.230	(−41.36)	−75.509	(−48.10)	−12.000	
YEAR2	1.996	(41.49)	0.019	(48.36)	0.003	
R2(F)	.642	(422.00)	.833	(1175.00)	.289	

NOTE: t values in parentheses.

	IROADL		INIA		INCA	
(5.51)	9604	(6.30)	12216	(6.61)	−407	(3.46)
(−4.94)	0.000	(2.41)	0.000	(0.09)	−0.000	(−10.13)
(−3.14)	−3.210	(−2.35)	4.296	(2.60)	−0.061	(−0.58)
(10.03)	0.633	(5.31)	0.593	(4.09)	0.018	(1.99)
(3.96)	0.000	(3.87)	0.000	(2.65)	−0.000	(−8.76)
(−0.70)	−0.001	(−2.53)	−0.001	(−17.60)	−0.000	(−6.65)
(2.85)	−11.855	(−11.24)	0.451	(0.35)	−0.262	(−3.21)
(3.47)	0.893	(0.56)	−11.598	(−6.04)	0.692	(5.66)
(4.61)	0.000	(0.40)	−0.001	(−3.29)	0.000	(6.52)
(−5.04)	0.001	(15.17)	−0.000	(0.02)	−0.000	(−6.01)
(1.87)	0.006	(10.28)	0.003	(4.23)	−0.000	(−10.96)
(2.92)	−0.006	(−4.12)	−0.001	(−5.72)	0.000	(4.68)
(−4.88)	3.688	(6.89)	1.681	(2.59)	0.115	(2.78)
(1.77)	1.859	(1.82)	0.402	(0.32)	−0.264	(−3.34)
(−1.47)	−0.960	(−2.85)	−0.856	(−2.10)	0.043	(1.64)
(1.92)	−0.671	(−4.29)	0.233	(1.23)	0.036	(2.94)
(−0.79)	0.506	(2.96)	0.664	(3.20)	0.062	(4.69)
(5.74)	0.417	(2.56)	−0.719	(−3.65)	0.044	(3.49)
(4.36)	0.548	(4.19)	1.257	(7.92)	−0.008	(−0.78)
(1.97)	0.213	(1.75)	0.080	(0.54)	0.009	(0.93)
(12.33)	0.088	(0.52)	0.613	(3.02)	0.052	(4.00)
(8.63)	0.729	(5.59)	−0.097	(−0.61)	0.002	(0.23)
(8.77)	0.144	(0.90)	0.688	(3.56)	0.008	(0.67)
(−5.57)	−9.838	(−6.36)	−12.510	(−6.67)	0.409	(3.42)
(5.62)	0.003	(6.41)	0.003	(6.72)	−0.000	(−3.38)
(96.00)	.328	(112.00)	.299	(100.00)	.264	(84.00)

TABLE B-2 Stage II Real Wages and Rent Estimates, All India and North India

Dependent Variables	All India		North India	
	IRWAGE	RENT	IRWAGE	IRENT
INTERCEPT	5374 (22.58)	-425564 (-2.83)	3391 (4.46)	5981 (1.47)
IOUT-IN	-0.018 (-0.63)	-23.208 (-1.27)	-0.292 (-1.25)	0.754 (0.60)
ISOUT-IN	0.054 (0.86)	114.201 (2.85)	0.230 (0.64)	-0.551 (-0.22)
INOUT-IN	0.046 (0.84)	-99.825 (-2.86)	-1.346 (-2.67)	1.157 (0.43)
IFOUT-IN	0.045 (0.90)	-15.475 (-0.48)	0.142 (0.30)	-2.921 (-1.16)
MSFDEN	0.000 (2.92)	-0.022 (-2.04)	-0.000 (-2.52)	0.001 (1.07)
IMSPDEN	-0.225 (-5.43)	5.432 (0.21)	-0.293 (-1.12)	3.010 (2.16)
NIAI	-0.505 (-3.76)	-32.898 (-0.39)	0.944 (2.66)	2.612 (1.37)
MKTS	0.022 (6.92)	-0.602 (-0.29)	0.070 (4.86)	0.342 (4.48)
LITERACY	-1.036 (-4.49)	74.026 (0.51)	-0.618 (-0.54)	-4.302 (-0.70)
ROADL	0.000 (1.68)	0.001 (0.14)	-0.001 (-3.88)	-0.003 (-3.67)
IADP	-0.054 (-2.90)	0.288 (0.02)	-0.074 (-1.65)	-0.038 (-0.15)
WHYV	0.139 (0.75)	113.632 (0.97)	0.634 (0.97)	-3.442 (-0.99)
OUTINNIA	0.077 (1.57)	12.890 (0.41)	0.638 (4.45)	3.172 (4.13)
OUTINFOP	-0.000 (-1.38)	0.004 (1.02)	0.000 (1.81)	-0.000 (-1.29)
OUTINMKT	0.007 (5.57)	0.922 (1.15)	0.016 (3.57)	-0.030 (-1.26)
OUTINLIT	-0.059 (-0.53)	-6.569 (-0.09)	-0.519 (-1.40)	-1.623 (-0.82)
OUTINRDA	-0.000 (-4.26)	-0.007 (-2.38)	-0.000 (-2.70)	-0.000 (-1.97)
NIAPOP	0.000 (2.14)	0.013 (1.26)	-0.000 (-5.06)	-0.001 (-2.97)
MKISPOP	-0.000 (-5.86)	0.000 (0.76)	-0.000 (-3.92)	-0.000 (-5.72)
LITPOP	0.000 (0.99)	0.017 (1.14)	-0.000 (-1.28)	-0.001 (-0.79)
ROADPOP	-5.109 (-0.40)	5.730 (0.71)	1.143 (4.20)	8.136 (5.72)
WHYUPOP	0.000 (5.66)	-0.028 (-2.46)	0.000 (2.12)	0.001 (2.08)
WHYVNIA	0.023 (0.24)	-158.193 (-2.64)	-0.062 (-0.21)	-0.656 (-0.42)
WHYMKT	0.007 (2.66)	-1.073 (-0.68)	0.018 (1.96)	0.154 (3.16)
WHYVLIT	-1.766 (-6.66)	-290.020 (-1.73)	-2.098 (-2.81)	-12.811 (-3.20)

WHYVROAD	0.000	(1.90)	0.009	(1.56)	-0.000	(-0.18)	0.000	(0.59)
HYVOUTIN	0.002	(0.01)	159.728	(2.32)	-0.322	(-1.32)	1.422	(1.09)
NIAOUTIN	0.112	(1.03)	-141.986	(-2.06)	-0.758	(-2.49)	-1.168	(-0.72)
MKTOUTIN	-0.019	(-7.99)	-0.900	(-0.58)	-0.039	(-4.31)	-0.093	(-1.90)
LITOUTIN	1.019	(5.07)	-108.569	(-0.85)	1.848	(2.75)	8.389	(2.33)
ROAOUTIN	0.000	(6.25)	0.002	(0.24)	1.802	(1.80)	0.001	(1.69)
MKTNOUTN	-0.002	(-0.83)	0.236	(0.14)	-0.008	(-1.01)	0.001	(0.02)
NIANOUTN	0.292	(3.04)	118.065	(1.95)	0.260	(1.05)	-0.926	(-0.69)
ROANOUTN	-0.000	(-5.44)	0.000	(0.04)	0.000	(1.99)	-0.000	(-0.63)
MSPOPISP	-0.000	(-8.41)	0.001	(0.12)	-0.000	(-1.58)	-0.000	(-0.66)
MSPOPINP	0.000	(7.76)	0.006	(0.50)	0.001	(4.47)	-0.000	(-0.00)
MSFOPIFP	-0.000	(-3.39)	-0.001	(-0.13)	-0.000	(-0.66)	0.001	(1.01)
YEAR	-5.464	(-22.60)	432.102	(2.83)	-3.441	(-4.44)	-6.028	(-1.45)
YEAR2	0.001	(22.63)	-0.110	(-2.83)	0.001	(4.43)	0.002	(1.44)
AGRO2	-0.079	(-3.72)	-5.781	(-0.43)				
AGRO3	-0.167	(-10.02)	-1.68	(-0.16)	0.166	(-7.52)	0.031	(0.26)
AGRO4	-0.064	(-4.90)	-0.110	(-0.13)				
AGRO5	-0.056	(-2.87)	3.858	(0.32)				
AGRO6	-0.076	(-5.34)	37.360	(4.16)				
R2(F)	.176	(55.00)	.024	(36.00)	.404	(30.00)	.148	(7.60)

NOTE: t values in parentheses.

7

Mauritius: Population and Land Use

Wolfgang Lutz and Einar Holm

Mauritius has one of the highest population densities of any sovereign territory in the world (presently about 590 persons/km^2 with a population of 1.1 million). In the 1950s and early 1960s Mauritius experienced very high rates of natural population growth (peaking at 3.5 percent per year) followed by a very steep decline in fertility that was probably the most rapid in the world. The total fertility rate dropped from 6.2 children per woman in 1963 to 3.4 in 1971. Currently, because of its young age structure, the population is still growing by 1 percent annually despite subreplacement fertility in the mid-1980s.

The fertility decline in Mauritius occurred in the absence of economic growth and may be attributed mostly to improved female educational status and active family planning programs (Lutz, 1990). During the 1970s gross national product (GNP) per capita started to increase slowly as a consequence of improvements in sugar cane yields, which was the primary product of the economy. The big boom in export-oriented industry, especially textiles, came later, in the 1980s, when for some years Mauritius even experienced double-digit growth rates in its GNP. As a consequence of this growth in labor-intensive industries, unemployment, which had been very high, entirely disappeared. The tourist sector also expanded rapidly during the past decade. As a consequence of this rapid development in the absence of any land use plan or government environmental policies, questions about the state of the Mauritian environment are becoming increasingly important.

Before the first known settlements in the seventeenth century, the is-

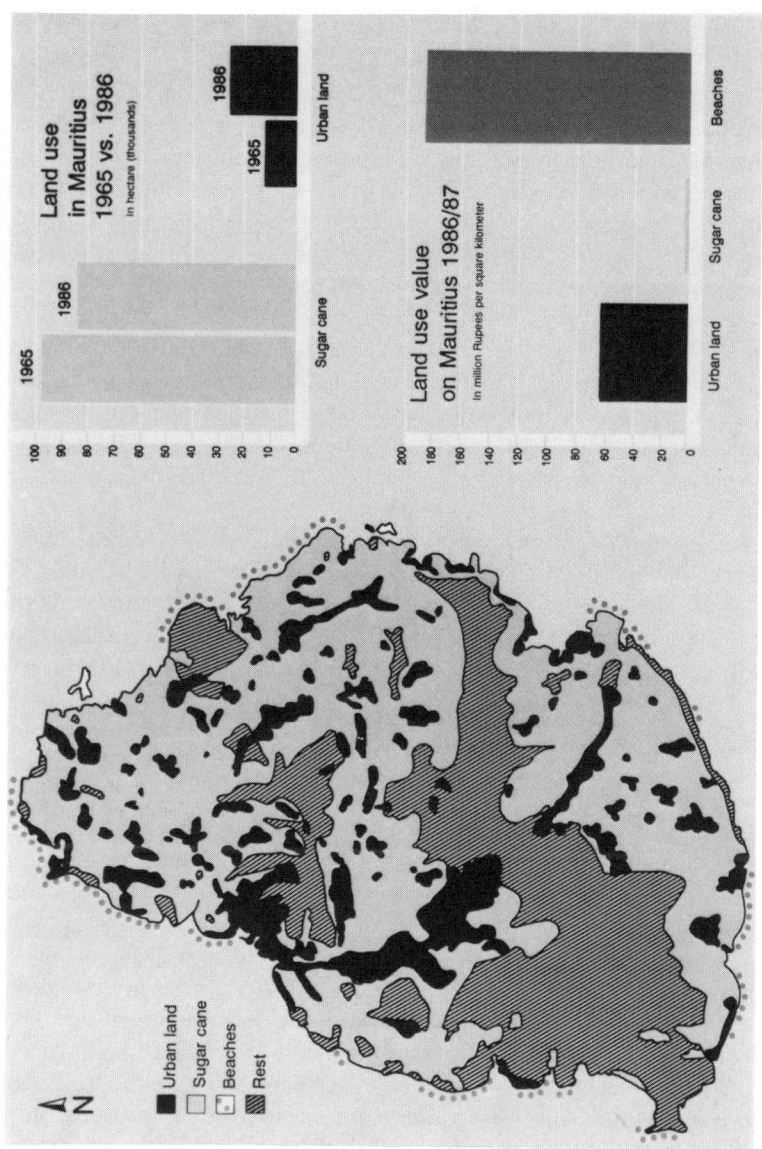

FIGURE 1 Map of land use patterns in Mauritius 1986-1987 and value added per Km^2 (in million rupees). SOURCE: Lutz (1991). Reprinted with permission.

land was largely covered by natural forest with considerable numbers of ebony trees. The deforestation of this valuable resource started the transformation of the landscape. A century later the growing of sugar cane was introduced and later became the spatially dominating economic land use on the island.

This gradual cultivation of forests and grasslands, etc., for sugar cane production culminated during the twentieth century. In 1965, 53 percent of all land on the island was used for growing sugar cane. Only 4 percent of the land was used for growing other agricultural products. For a long time, Mauritius imported at least two-thirds of its food for consumption (foodcrops, livestock, and poultry).

As can be seen from Figure 1, the main change in land use since 1965 is the transformation of sugar cane land into urban space. The area used for growing sugar cane decreased by 15 percent from 1965 to 1986, to cover 45 percent of the total land area of the island. Meanwhile, urban land use increased by 215 percent, thereby significantly increasing its share of the total island land use. Compared to that, other land use changes are minor, although economically significant. Tea production lost one-third of its former area, whereas land used for the production of food crops increased by 50 percent to 1.6 percent of the total land area.

Another significant change demanding small but very scarce land resources is the rapid growth, especially in the late 1980s, of the tourist industry. It is estimated that some 50 hotels on the beach now occupy almost 30 km of the coastline, or about 2.9 km^2. This is a small amount of total island land space, but not much more of its kind is available. This land use also competes directly with land use for recreational purposes, i.e., public beaches.

Usually, one implicit assumption inherent in the study of the relationship between population and land use change is the existence of a strong, direct relationship between the amount of arable land available and the number of people that can be supported by the agricultural production of that area, i.e., the carrying capacity constraint of a society mainly occupied with hunting, collecting, or growing of crops and livestock for its own consumption. However, this direct relationship changes character and becomes weaker as a country develops and as it enters international markets. New agricultural technology and especially the substitution of agriculture for other economic activities increases the "yield" per unit of land considerably and thereby the carrying capacity. Therefore, it is essential to consider not only agriculture but the spatial requirements for all kinds of human activities when discussing land use change and the relationship between population change and land use.

Comparing value added and space requirements reveals that rural land use produces less than 3 million rupees (MRs) per square kilometer whereas the economic activities on the total coastal strip (100 m from the water-

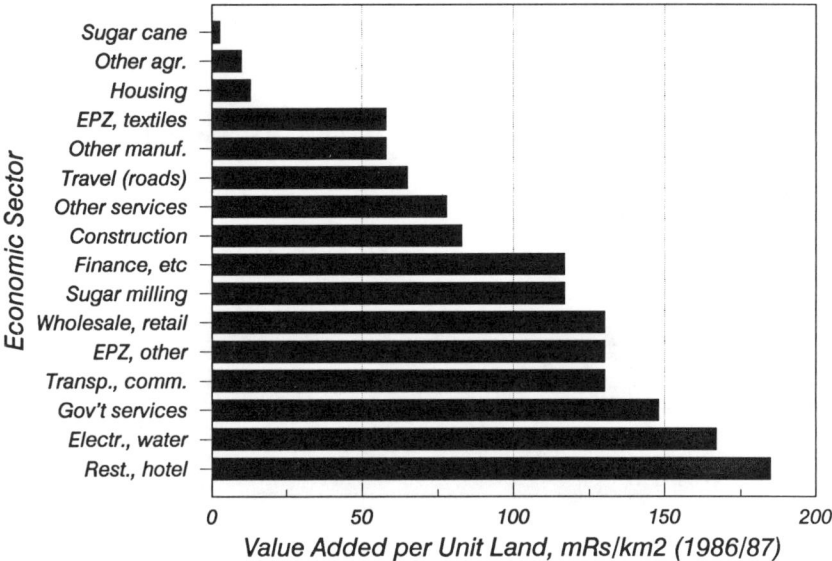

FIGURE 2 Value added per land unit on Mauritius by economic sector.

front) can be valued at 185 MRs/km^2 and the different urban activities create values on the order of 64 MRs/km^2. Those figures allude to the strength of the economic forces propelling the conversion of rural land for use by industry, urbanization, and export activities during the development process.

Figure 2 gives a more detailed picture of the production of value per land unit by different sectors. The figure is also more speculative in its detailed assumptions. The main tendency is quite clear: Other agriculture produces more value per land unit than does sugar cane production; and the consumption value of residential housing is higher compared to any agricultural use of the same land, but considerably lower than all commercial urban land use. Within the urban category, industrial sites produce somewhat less value per land unit compared to private and public services. Two nonurban land use activities are at the level of industry and services: commercial and private use of road infrastructure and tourist hotels (mainly on the beaches). On Mauritius, their production of value added per land unit exceeds all other land use categories, including the urban ones.

The ratio of value added per land unit between the extremes, tourist hotels and sugar cane, is 70 to 1. On average, urban activities produce at least 20 times more per land unit as compared to rural activities. With such variations it is obvious that rankings of used land area (Figure 3) versus the absolute value produced or consumed in that land area will differ (Figure

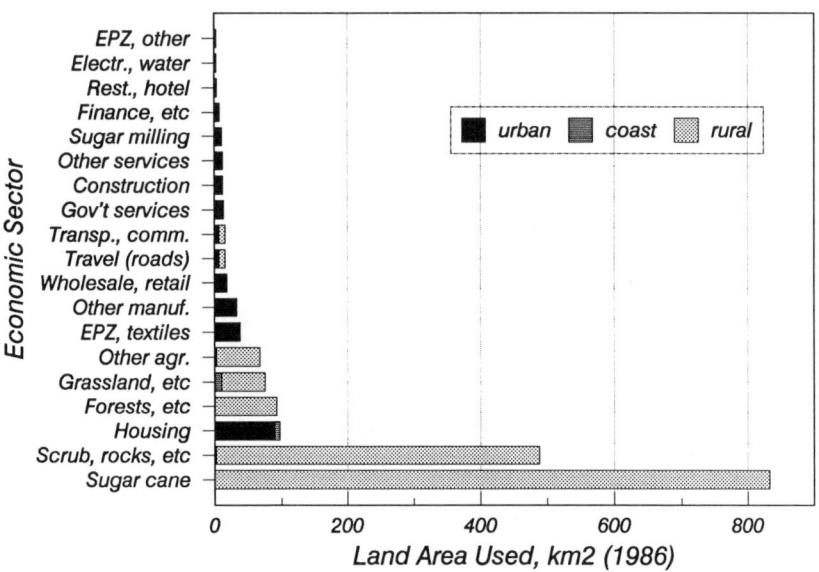

FIGURE 3 Land area used on Mauritius by economic sector and land use type.

4). About 80 percent of the value produced or consumed is based on activities that take place on 10 percent of the land area. Only sugar cane production still rates high both in the amount of land used and the absolute value added of its production.

This simple relationship between value added and used land is only a crude indicator of the direction and strength of the economic forces driving changes in the land use pattern. If everything else is equal this relation would serve as an estimate of the land rent. But everything else is not equal. The amounts and costs of capital and labor, the two other production factors besides land, vary considerably among production sectors.

For example, although other types of agriculture (e.g., consumption crops, tea, flowers, etc.) produce almost 3 times as much value added per land unit as sugar cane, they are not necessarily the more profitable land use because the labor requirements for producing food crops, for example, are much higher compared to those of sugar cane growing. If the level of income per capita, and thereby of wages is high enough, and if the land is not required for other (e.g., urban), more profitable activities, then extensive sugar production still is the more profitable land use alternative.

Judged from a traditional carrying capacity concept, Mauritius, with its very high population density, could be expected to be in trouble. It would not be easy to feed its population at the present level of consumption per

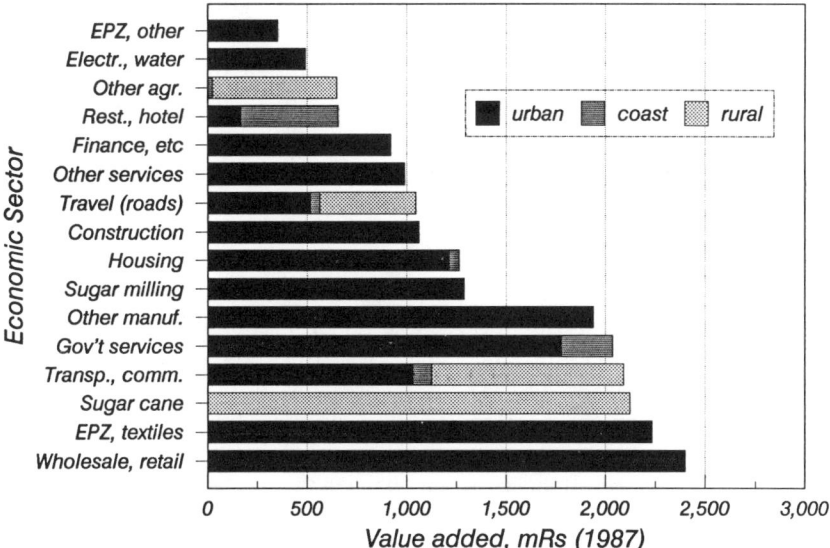

FIGURE 4 Value added on Mauritius by economic sector and land use type.

capita using traditional agriculture. Obviously, the present economic base of Mauritius is not a traditional agricultural one but rather is that of an urban society with export industry and services as its main means of production.

Perhaps Mauritius never was a subsistence economy. Ebony, sugar, spices, textiles, and tourist services are all export products. In traditional agriculture one produces goods for immediate domestic consumption. Sugar cane has, since long before the reduction in fertility and the economic growth of recent decades, dominated agricultural land use on Mauritius. From a subsistence point of view sugar cane production and sugar milling are more similar to an export industry than to domestic agriculture. The whole purpose of export-oriented production is to get a valuable asset for use in trading on the world market, thereby importing what otherwise had to be produced locally for domestic consumption. Therefore it is not the direct need for food crops, etc., to feed a growing population that steers land use patterns on Mauritius, but rather the desire for an efficient total production and consumption pattern.

Still, at any level of economic development, sufficient quantities of food have to be produced somewhere. The question for a small region or country is why do it themselves, domestically? Suppose it would be feasible to increase the present level of food self-sufficiency from one-third to almost 100 percent by converting, say, another 2-4 percent of the total land area from sugar cane production to other types of agriculture while at the same time increasing interline cropping within the sugar fields, corresponding to still another 2-4 percent of land for food production.

Due to most evaluations of the profitability of food crops versus sugar cane, the alternative of sugar cane (or industrial or tourist) production on that land would have created resources to buy both the food needed and other goods and services on the world market. So why not continue to explore the relative economic advantages for production and land use that have evolved based on sugar, tourism, textiles, and electronics? Other factors will be important to a move toward agricultural self-sufficiency, such as lower sensitivity to world market changes, possible negative environmental consequences of sugar cane or textile production, or possible cultural and political reasons. The task for the Mauritian government is to find the right balance between profitability, political feasibility, and longer term resilience.

In general, causal effects between changes in population and changes in land use and per capita land availability may go in both directions. Changes in population size, structure, and regional distribution may influence changes in the use of the available land. On the other hand, a clearly visible shortage of land may induce the population to limit its growth. There is some evidence that this factor played a role in the rapid fertility decline in Mauritius.

This paper draws from a larger study on population and sustainable development in Mauritius conducted by the International Institute for Applied Systems Analysis in scientific collaboration with the University of Mauritius and with funding from the United Nations Population Fund. With the help of a computer simulation and information system, the project studies the effect of changes in population size and structure (by age, sex, educational status, and labor force participation) on the economy and, in turn, on two environmental systems, namely water dynamics and land use. The model assures that all links between population and land use work through the social and economic system and that there are no immediate effects due to population changes (Lutz and Toth, 1991).

Sometimes changes in land use directly conflict. Clearly, the same piece of land cannot be used for sugar cane production and urban settlements at the same time. An industrial site on the beach effectively prevents its use for tourism. Other types of land use can coexist, more or less symbiotically, like the method of sugar cane production known as interline cropping, whereby full use is made of the rotation land between two cane cycles. A decentralized settlement pattern might coexist with small-scale production of food crops. The chance to partly substitute food imports with local production of such food crops and the vision of making Mauritius a "garden island" makes this possibility attractive. On the other hand, the economies of growing food crops as compared to sugar cane are uncertain, and a decentralized settlement pattern increases the volume of private transport needed and thereby the import of cars and fuel, as well as the amount of air pollution (Holm and Oberg, 1991).

The constraints on changing land use are partly physical. There is not much unused land left with soil and surface structures suitable for any kind of agricultural use. The same holds for the availability of new beaches for development of the tourism. Hence, like in many other places in the world, the question is not one of conquering virgin land, but rather how best to set up a useful garden scheme that takes maximum advantage of all available land.

In Mauritius, the effects of population growth on land use are highly indirect. Changes in the size and structure of the population do not automatically result in more or less agricultural land because through its integration in the world market, Mauritius can buy what it needs if it has the assets. Hence, land use changes are driven by profitability considerations in combination with certain government policies. If there is any direct effect of population growth, then it might be the increased demand for housing. Indeed, the expansion of urban areas in Mauritius has been associated not only with an increase in the number of people, but also with an increase in the number of square meters of living space per person due to increased wealth. Such an association, however, holds only under constant housing patterns. A transition to high-rise buildings—as is presently happening—will change the effect of population growth on urban land use.

A much more detailed discussion of the population-development-environment interactions in Mauritian history and in its future (up to 2050) partly using the Mauritius computer simulation model is given in Lutz (1993). In conclusion, one can say that, through its social and economic development, Mauritius is in a position to have some freedom of choice in its future land use changes.

REFERENCES

Holm, E., and S. Oberg
    1991   Aspects of geographical distribution on a small island: future settlement patterns in Mauritius, cost and benefits. Pp. 311-325 in W. Lutz and F.L. Toth eds., *Population, Economy, and Environment in Mauritius*. CP-91-1 Laxenburg, Austria: International Institute for Applied Systems Analysis.

Lutz, W.
    1990   Population and sustainable development. *POPNET* 18(Fall):1-4.
    1991   Population, environment, and development: a case study of Mauritius. *Options* (December):11-15.
    1993   *Population-Development-Environment: Understanding Interactions in Mauritius*. London: Springer-Verlag.

Lutz, W., and F.L. Toth, eds.
    1991   *Population, Economy, and Environment in Mauritius*. CP-91-1. Laxenburg, Austria: International Institute for Applied Systems Analysis.

8

Honduras: Population, Inequality, and Resource Destruction

Billie R. DeWalt, Susan C. Stonich, and Sarah L. Hamilton

The population of Honduras in 1989 was estimated at 4.98 million people, nearly double the 1970 population of 2.63 million. During the same period, the country experienced environmental destruction on a grand scale. Soil erosion, watershed deterioration, deforestation, and destruction of coastal resources occurred at alarming rates. Based on appearances, there seems to be a direct link between the rapid population increase and this nonsustainable utilization of land and water resources. The purpose of this case study is to examine the evidence concerning population increase and natural resource destruction to determine whether there is such a direct link.

The accumulated evidence concerning southern Honduras is remarkably consistent in showing that environmental destruction is attributable more to the inequality of resource distribution and patterns of economic development in the region rather than to population increase. Although our evidence relates primarily to Honduras, it appears that these same processes have also been characteristic of other Central American countries and that they have played a major role in causing the violent conflicts and environmental difficulties that characterize the region today (see Williams, 1986; Leonard, 1987).

HONDURAS: AN OVERVIEW

With an area of 43,277 mi^2 (a bit larger than the state of Kentucky), Honduras is the second largest of the Central American republics. Over 80 percent of the land is mountainous, a physical feature that contributes to the relative isolation of some areas of the country.

Honduras is predominantly an agricultural country. In 1980, 60 percent of the population was directly involved in agriculture (World Bank, 1991:297), and in 1987 agriculture accounted for 83 percent of the value of merchandise exports. The major exports in order of importance were bananas, coffee and cacao, fish and shellfish, wood products, fruits, nuts, flowers, sugar, and livestock products.

Southern Honduras is more dependent on agriculture than is the rest of the country. Approximately 70 percent of its population is directly dependent on agriculture for their livelihood. For this reason, changes in land utilization patterns in the region have an immediate and discernible effect.

THE POPULATION SITUATION

Although the total fertility rate for Honduras dropped from 7.4 in 1970 to 5.4 in 1989, and the annual growth rate declined from 3.71 percent (1981-1982) to 2.96 percent (1988-1989), the country's population continues to grow rapidly. Population density has climbed from 12.2 persons/km^2 in 1950 to 35.6 in 1985 (see Stonich, 1986:145).

This population expansion has occurred in a nation characterized by extreme inequality of wealth[1] and one of the lowest per capita incomes in Latin America (Sheahan, 1987). Additionally, Honduras exhibits one of the highest rates of rural destitution in Latin America (57-75 percent, depending on the measures used, in the 1970s). Unequal distribution of resources between rural and urban populations and within the rural sector means that more than 70 percent of rural families lived on less than $20 per month in 1980 (CSPE/OEA, 1982).

Honduras has been designated a "food priority country" by the United Nations. Per capita domestic food production has declined; Honduras has been a net importer of maize, rice, sorghum, and beans since 1976. In 1975, the prevalence of second- and third-degree malnutrition was 38 percent (Teller et al., 1979), and over 70 percent of children under 5 years of age suffered from some form of protein-calorie malnutrition during the 1970s (SAPLAN, 1981). In the late 1980s, the *average* energy deficit in rural areas was approximately 20 percent (USAID Honduras, 1989a).

---

[1]The top 20 percent of the population held 68 percent of the wealth in the 1970s, compared with 58 percent in Mexico and 50 percent in Argentina (Sheahan, 1987).

CHANGING LAND USE PATTERNS IN THE SOUTH

Southern Honduras experienced a substantial expansion of commercial agriculture in the years immediately following World War II. The Honduran government became an active agent of development, creating a variety of state institutions and agencies to expand government services, modernize the country's financial system, and undertake infrastructural projects.

This period of intensified public sector investments coincided with temporary high prices on the world market for primary commodities like cotton, coffee, and cattle. Large landowners in the south who had access to the good lands on the coastal plain had historically been unable to respond to favorable economic conditions because of the lack of necessary infrastructure such as transportation, markets, and credit. With the infrastructure in place these owners found it profitable to expand production for the global market.

The Cotton Boom

It was cotton cultivation that first transformed traditional social patterns of production in southern Honduras (Stares, 1972:35; White, 1977; Durham, 1979:119; Boyer, 1983:91). In the late 1940s and 1950s, people from El Salvador began commercial cultivation of cotton in Honduras.[2] As in El Salvador and Nicaragua, commercial production involves considerable mechanization in land preparation, planting, cultivation, and aerial spraying. Cotton cultivation along the Pacific coastal plain also is dependent on

---

[2]In 1969, the Government of Honduras expelled several thousand Salvadoran immigrants, many of whom had lived in Honduras for over a generation. El Salvador retaliated by invading Honduras. This so-called Soccer War (because it occurred shortly after the soccer teams representing the countries competed in World Cup qualifying matches) was widely attributed to "population pressure"—the competition of poor Hondurans and Salvadorans for increasingly scarce arable land. Many analysts concluded that a Malthusian scenario was being played out in which the population had exceeded the carrying capacity of the land.

Durham's (1979) classic analysis of this situation demonstrated that it was the use and distribution of land, rather than its carrying capacity, that resulted in the problems of food production and the inability of families to meet subsistence needs. Durham found that the landless and land-poor agriculturalists unable to rent land in El Salvador made up most of the migrant stream to Honduras. Mostly renters and sharecroppers, the Salvadorans' access to land depended on the decisions of large landholders rather than on competition with Honduran smallholders. In fact, immigrants and poor Honduran farmers joined forces to challenge a large hacienda owner who attempted to incorporate national lands into his estate. Durham concluded that the land base of poor farmers decreased to the point of threatening survival only partly as a result of population increase. As he put it, "Land use patterns show that land is not scarce for large landholders" (1979:54).

the heavy use of chemical inputs (especially insecticides and fertilizers). The indiscriminate use of pesticides in the cotton growing regions remains one of the most pervasive environmental contamination and human health problems throughout Central America. Water from cotton growing areas shows heavy contamination from DDT, Dieldrin, Toxaphene, and Parathion (USAID, 1982), and the results of a 1981 study to determine the levels of pesticide poisoning in the area around the city of Choluteca revealed that approximately 10 percent of the inhabitants had pesticide levels sufficiently high to be considered cases of intoxication (Leonard, 1987:149). The land and water contamination from pesticides, as well as high levels of pesticide residues in food supplies, have had substantial effects on human health (Williams, 1986; Leonard, 1987).

Following the boom and bust cycles of the international cotton market, the amount of land in cotton in southern Honduras fluctuated considerably between the late 1940s and the late 1980s. The major social effect of the cotton boom was to increase inequalities in access to land. Large landowners revoked peasant tenancy or sharecropping rights, raised rental rates exorbitantly, and evicted peasants forcibly from national land or from land of undetermined tenure (Durham, 1979; Boyer, 1983:94). Thus, one of the effects of increased cotton cultivation was to displace many poor farmers from the most suitable agricultural lands in the south. Cotton also, however, provided a substantial number of seasonal jobs during the harvest season. The long staple cotton grown in the region was, and still is, largely picked by hand.

The Cattle Boom

The expansion of the cattle industry has probably had the most extensive and devastating environmental impact (DeWalt, 1983; 1986). Between 1960 and 1983, 57 percent of the total loan funds allocated by the World Bank for agriculture and rural development in Central America supported the production of beef for export. During that same period, Honduras obtained 51 percent of the total World Bank funds that were disbursed in Central America—of which 34 percent were for livestock projects (calculated from Table 4-1 in Jarvis, 1986:124).

These programs were all channeled into the region through the large landowners, merchants, and industrialists who made up the elites of the countries (DeWalt, 1986; Stonich and DeWalt, 1989). In a context of declining agricultural commodity prices, high labor costs, unreliable rainfall, and international and national support for livestock, landowners reallocated their land from cotton and/or grain cultivation to pasture for cattle. Cattle appealed to landowners in Honduras because it is a commodity that could be produced with very little labor. While it takes considerable human labor

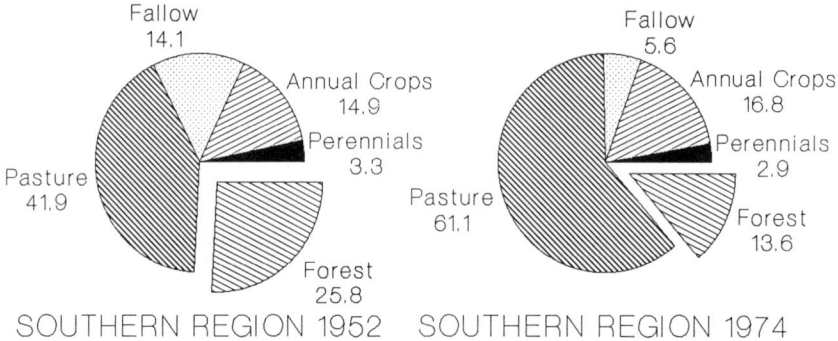

FIGURE 1: Changing land use patterns: southern Honduras, 1952-1974. (All figures are percentages.) SOURCE: DGECH (1954, 1976).

to produce sugar cane, cotton, melons, or coffee, with just two or three hired hands and extensive pasture it is possible to manage a herd of several hundred cattle.[3] In Honduras, land reform programs ironically also encouraged the expansion of pasture for livestock. Landowners who feared expropriation of unutilized fallow and forest land fenced it and planted pasture as a way of establishing use of the land without increasing labor inputs (DeWalt and DeWalt, 1982:69; Jarvis, 1986:157).

The main limitation to beef production is pastureland, and this is why there were such extensive changes in land use patterns in Honduras and the other Central American countries during the 1960s and 1970s. Expansion took place not only in the lowlands and foothills where cattle raising traditionally occurred, but also in the highlands where many of the wealthier peasant farmers augmented cattle production (Durham, 1979; Boyer, 1983; Stonich, 1986). Increased livestock production in the lowlands and the highlands also accelerated the expulsion of peasants from national and private lands (White, 1977:126-156; Stonich, 1986:139-143). Between 1952 and 1974, pasture in the region increased from 41.9 percent of the land to 61.1 (see Figure 1). Precipitous declines are evident in both fallow land and the amount of land in forest. This has resulted in significant increases in both soil erosion and deforestation.

Honduras is losing its soils at the rate of 10,000 ha per year and, if current trends continue, "the forest resource will be exhausted in a generation" (USAID Honduras 1990:3). Many of the best lands in the country are

---

[3]For example, it has been estimated that "coffee requires between 64 and 208 person days per year, while beef-cattle production requires only between 4 and 8" (Guess, 1979:48).

in pasture. The Central Bank estimated in August 1988 that 48 percent of the valley lands in Honduras—covering 31 principal valleys—are in pasture. Of these, 22 percent are located in the southern part of the country (USAID Honduras, 1990:10). While the livestock boom has ended in several of the other Central American countries, the number of cattle in Honduras continues to grow rapidly.

Cantaloupe and Shrimp

Because of a decline in demand for beef and falling prices, in the late 1980s capitalist investors in southern Honduras began investing in two new nontraditional export crops—cantaloupe and shrimp. During the 1980s, cantaloupe production expanded at a rate of 23 percent per year and shrimp production at a rate of 22 percent (USAID Honduras, 1990:2), and in 1989-1990 these two commodities contributed an estimated $25 million in export earnings to the Honduran economy (Meckenstock et al., 1991:4). These earnings have been offset by both environmental and social costs.

The area planted in cantaloupe is projected to reach 9,000 ha by 1996. On the positive side, cantaloupe production provides a substantial number of temporary jobs in production and in packing for export. Accompanying the boom in production, however, have been escalating levels of soil degradation, aphid-borne viruses, and insect pests like leaf miners and whiteflies. Even with two to three applications of pesticides a week, crop losses in 1989-1990 were 56 percent of harvest projections (Meckenstock et al., 1991:5). Runoff of pesticides poses a threat to community water supplies in the region as well as to the estuaries in the Gulf of Fonseca where shrimp farming has become a big business and where shrimp larvae already show relatively high levels of DDT.

The area in shrimp farms increased from about 100 hectares in 1982 to 11,515 hectares in 1992. The expansion of shrimp farms has occurred in areas of mud flats, beaches, and mangroves that were once public lands used by the rural poor for hunting, fishing, and the gathering of shellfish. Government concessions to shrimp companies have effectively turned these areas into private property. Twenty-year concessions have been granted to companies for 4 lempiras (less than $1) per hectare per year. Fences are erected, armed guards installed, and local people excluded from areas they had once freely utilized.

Parallels in the social process associated with the recent boom in shrimp mariculture and the earlier expansions of export commodities (cotton, sugar, and livestock) in the region are striking. Past "enclosure movements" in which small farmers were removed from relatively good agricultural land, often by force and with the compliance of local authorities, are being repeated on the intertidal lands. Intertidal land once open to public use for fishing, shellfish collecting, salt producing, and the cutting of firewood and tanbark is now being converted to private use. Concessions, guarantees of occupancy, and titles have been acquired by the firms involved in shrimp production. Conflicts have arisen among the large foreign-owned operations, local medium-scale entrepreneurs, and campesino cooperatives over access to estuaries, lagoons, and mangroves. Three fishermen died in incidents involving shrimp farms in 1991 and 1992.

Moreover, although development documents written in the mid-1980s stressed the importance of incorporating resource-poor households in the development process primarily through the formation and support of shrimp farming cooperatives (USAID, 1985), more recent reports conclude that only the larger, more intensive operations are profitable (USAID Honduras, 1989b). These large operations generate very few employment opportunities, typically employing fewer than one person per hectare (Gonzalez et al., 1987; cited in SECPLAN/DESFIL, 1989:179).

The construction of shrimp farms has also exacerbated the destruction of mangrove forests along the coast. This may eventually become as extensive as the mangrove destruction that occurred along the coast of Ecuador in connection with development of shrimp farming in that country (LACR, 1989).

Summary

During the last 40 years, the restructuring of agriculture in southern Honduras has impoverished both the landscape and an increasing percentage of the population.[4] The general trend has been toward resource oligopoly, patterns of exploitation and production that jeopardize future systemic sustainability in exchange for quick profits, wanton destruction of natural resources, and underemployment. None of these processes resulted, even indirectly, from population pressure.

---

[4] A recent report by agricultural scientists reported that: "Since the 1950s, the agricultural economy of southern Honduras has been dominated by a series of boom and bust cycles of export commodities. Cattle, cotton, and sugar have each reached their zenith only to dissipate in the face of declining productivity and adverse world markets. Much of this instability has been self-inflicted through degradation of the natural resource base which has reduced productivity and profitability. At present, non-traditional export crops like melon and shrimp are experiencing the great expectations and up-swing of this cycle; however, signs of limitations and stress on production are becoming apparent" (Meckenstock et al., 1991:2).

SMALLHOLDER AGRICULTURE

Until now, we have been talking about a relatively small percentage of producers, those with access to the best lands and the most resources. Indeed, as already implied, land distribution in Honduras is highly unequal. Table 1 compares the distribution of land in the municipality of Pespire in southern Honduras, and in the country as a whole.[5] Landholding patterns are remarkably consistent across local, regional, and national levels. Approximately two-thirds of producers have access to less than 5 ha of land; this multitude share only 9-10 percent of the total land area. In contrast, the 10-12 percent of the population with access to over 50 ha controls more than 50 percent of the land area. These are the commercial producers on whom the previous section focussed. The question remains, what is happening to the small producers, the majority of the population, as large commercial concerns expand?

Most small producers are concentrated on steep mountain slopes that are of marginal quality for agriculture (the brief descriptions below are based on three small communities we studied in the municipality of Pespire).[6] Although large landholdings are relatively rare in the communities studied

TABLE 1 Comparison of Inequality of Landholding in Pespire, in Southern Honduras, and in Honduras

Size of Holdings (ha)	Percentage of Farms			Percentage of Area		
	Pespire	South	Honduras	Pespire	South	Honduras
<5	63.4	68.4	63.9	10.1	10.3	9.1
5-9.9	15.9	13.6	14.5	9.9	8.1	7.7
10-19.9	9.8	8.8	9.8	12.2	10.4	10.2
20-49.9	7.4	6.0	7.8	19.6	14.8	17.5
50-99.9	2.2	1.7	2.3	12.8	9.5	11.5
≥100	1.3	1.6	1.7	35.3	46.8	44.0
Total no. of farms	1,714	25,412	195,341			
Total no. of ha.				19,383	304,462	2,629,859

---

[5]This inequality of land distribution is also found in the other Central American countries (see DeWalt and Bidegaray, 1991:24).

[6]See DeWalt and DeWalt (1982) for a report on the methodology and results of this research.

TABLE 2 Comparison of Land Tenure Characteristics in the Highland Communities Studied

Characteristics	Research Communities				
	1	2	3	4	5
Mean size of holdings (ha)	2.3	3.7	5.9	4.6	3.1
Maximum size of holdings	14	69	39	47	214
Percentage of landowners in community	63	27	46	72	—
Percentage with holdings of less than 1 ha	10	24	49	29	40
Percentage that purchased land	41	19	44	31	—

NOTE: Community 1 = San Antonio (Stonich, 1986); Community 2 = Esquimay (Stonich, 1986); Community 3 = Cacautare/El Naranjito (DeWalt and DeWalt, 1982); Community 4 = mean of villages in Langue (Durham, 1979); and Community 5 = mean of 7 communities (Boyer, 1983).

(see Table 2), there is considerable inequality in access to land among smallholders. The mean size of landholdings for all of the communities is quite small (less than 6 ha). While the percentage of surveyed households owning land ranges from 27 percent to 72 percent by community (see Table 2), a large percentage of people in all communities are landless or have access to less than one ha of land. In the villages around Cacautare, 54 percent of the sample rented, borrowed, or sharecropped land, generally in quantities smaller than 5 manzanas (less than 3.45 ha).[7] Most landowners had access to less than 7 ha of land. Only two individuals held more than 28 ha, with the largest being about 39 ha.

In these communities, landowners and renters generally practice some form of shifting cultivation[8] that involves interplanting maize and sorghum.

---

[7]Similarly, 55 percent of sampled households in villages around Esquimay rent, borrow, or sharecrop land (Stonich, 1986:202). Durham (1979:144) reports that 39.4 percent of people in Langue rent land; he does not measure borrowing or sharecropping arrangements.

[8]Although the type of cultivation that is practiced by small farmers in southern Honduras is usually described as slash-and-burn agriculture, the way that a field enters the cultivation cycle is more accurately described as a slash-and-mulch system. Here, the secondary forest growth is cut down, but rather than being burned it is left lying on the ground to serve as mulch for the grain crops that are planted.

The first year of cultivation of a plot of hillside land in Cacautare usually begins with a slash-and-mulch system in which maize or sorghum is planted. When planting maize, all brush, vines, and weeds are cut down in August.[9] A digging stick is used to plant maize among the decaying vegetation. After the maize has germinated, the larger trees are felled and left in the field. When sorghum is planted, the seeds are broadcast-sown under second growth forest; then the trees, brush, and weeds are cut. In both cropping systems, the decaying vegetation is left in the field as a mulch. In the second (and sometimes third) year of cultivation, the now-dry brush and trees are burned in April and maize and sorghum are interplanted.[10] In the past, much of this land would then be allowed to lie fallow for a long period of time to recover its fertility. Now, however, an increasing proportion of the land, especially among larger landowners, is being converted to pasture. As Figure 1 showed, the percentage of land in pasture in the south of Honduras expanded by half in only 20 years, and at the expense of forest and fallow land.

Landless peasants provide the labor required to convert land to pasture in exchange for temporary but inexpensive land rental. Poor peasants in Cacautare had relatively little difficulty renting land in the early 1980s. The rental cost of 1 manzana of land in 1981 was only about $8, with the renter agreeing to leave the crop residue in the field. While haulm used for grazing animals in the dry season was worth up to $50 per manzana, rental costs still seemed relatively low.

Landowners are willing to rent their land cheaply because the most expensive and labor-intensive aspect of hillside agriculture is clearing secondary growth forest. Rather than paying laborers to cut brush and trees, landowners rent their land to the landless for a year or two. Part of the rental agreement is that pasture grasses will be sown in the field between rows of subsistence crops so that the landowner will be left with a new pasture. We estimate that this arrangement saves the landowner at least $100 in labor costs for each hectare of new pasture (see DeWalt and DeWalt, 1982).

Why are landowners more interested in growing pasture to feed livestock than in growing basic grains or export crops (cf. Parsons, 1976:126)?

---

[9]This period is known as the *postrera*; it occurs after the end of the dry period (*canicula*) that often falls within the middle of the rainy season.

[10] From an agronomic point of view this system seems odd because these plants compete for the same nutrients in the soil. From the farmers' point of view, however, the system makes a great deal of sense. The maize is a rapidly maturing variety that can be harvested in between 60 and 70 days (around the middle of July). This is the period of the year when the previous year's grain harvest has been depleted, and, although maize yields are small, they do sustain the farmer for a few months during the remainder of the cropping season. The sorghum intercrop is left in the field to mature and is not harvested until December.

The main reason is that the potential return on investment from 1 manzana of grain in the harsh, risky environment of southern Honduras is minimal. In the best case scenario (i.e., highest market price, lowest input prices), farmers are able to make a profit of only about $75 per manzana (DeWalt, 1985:177-178). This potential profit is not enough to entice most larger landowners to produce grain beyond what they require for their own consumption.[11]

For farmers with sufficient land, there is a much more lucrative option available in raising livestock.[12] Several of the relatively well-off smallholders with whom we spoke in Cacautare reported that they had little interest in planting sorghum and maize because they were not profitable crops. They said that market prices were too low, labor costs had climbed, laborers no longer worked as hard as they did in the past, and the weather, insects, and other natural forces made grain harvests too unpredictable. Our calculations indicate that their average profit from selling one steer exceeded the total profit from several manzanas of grain. As a result, the 12 largest landowners in our sample had begun converting significant portions of their land into pasture.[13]

The environmental result of pasture expansion and land concentration is substantial pressure on the land-resource base and its degradation. Farmers in Cacautare reported that fields *should* be cultivated for only 3 years in a row (mean = 2.93, range = 1 to 5 years) and *should* lie fallow for at least 6 years (mean = 6.22, range = 1 to 15 years). Both Stonich (1986, in press) and Durham (1979) demonstrate a direct relationship between the size of landholdings and the amount of time fields lie fallow. Table 3 shows this relationship for the highland villages around Esquimay. Farmers with over

---

[11]Those farmers with small landholdings or those who are landless do have an incentive to produce their own grain. Much of the investment put into the production of crops is their own labor; thus their own cash inputs are relatively minimal. In addition, if they had to purchase grain at retail prices, this would involve a significant outlay of cash.

[12]The importance of cattle raising for farmers in the region, however, can be gauged from the number of sales of animals recorded in the year prior to our research by the 52 persons we sampled. Thirteen individuals had sold cattle, and 37 animals changed hands. These animals were sold for amounts ranging from 250 to 500 lempiras each ($125-250). Profits from selling even one animal thus exceed the total amount of profits that might be gained from cultivating several manzanas of grain.

[13]Even some of the small landowners with whom we talked expressed fears about the government expropriating their land to be redistributed. One way that farmers felt they could be assured of retaining their land would be to demonstrate that they were productively utilizing it. Forest land, even if it is fallow and will be cultivated in the future, appears not to be in use. So some farmers reported that an additional incentive for planting pasture was that it showed that their land was being used in case another series of land reform programs were promulgated.

TABLE 3 Agricultural Practices by Land-Tenure and Farm Size in Southern Highland Villages, 1983

Type of Tenancy	N	Percentage of Land in Food Crops[a]	Percentage of Land in Pasture	Mean No. of Cattle Owned (range)	Length of Fallow (yr)
Renters[b]	74	95	—	0.17 (0-4)	2.7
Owners					
<1 ha[c]	23	80	—	0.22 (0-3)	2.7
1-4.9 ha	87	51	4	0.22 (0-3)	3.2
5-19.9 ha	15	23	21	2.5 (0-13)	3.8
20-50 ha	5	6	48	8.0 (7-9)	5.0
>50 ha	1	6	20[d]	50.0 (50)	6.0

[a]Maize, sorghum, and beans.
[b]Mean area of rented land = 1.4 ha.
[c]Of the owners, 51 percent also rent land.
[d]The largest landowner rents additional grazing land in the lowlands.

SOURCE: Stonich (1989:287).

20 ha allow their land to lie fallow for 5 to 6 years. Those with less land resume cultivation of their land after it has been fallow for only 2 or 3 years (cf. Durham, 1979:144-45). Boyer (1983) reports that in other communities in the south, a fallow period is no longer part of the agricultural system.

Increasing intensity of land use means that yields are much lower, soil fertility is rapidly depleted, and soil erosion is exacerbated. Lack of vegetation on the hillsides also causes frequent landslides when torrential rains hit the region.

For the land-poor, the expansion of pasture threatens not only the fertility of the land but also its availability. Their dilemma was succinctly expressed by one of our informants:

> Right now we have land available to rent, but each year you can see the land in forest disappearing. In a few years, it will all be pasture and there will be no land available to rent. How are we to produce for our families then? We see what is happening, but we have no choice because our families have to eat now.

POPULATION GROWTH AND LAND USE CHANGES

Southern Honduras is the most densely settled region of the country; it comprises only 5 percent of the total area of the country but contains approximately 11 percent of the population. Population density increased from 29.8 persons/km^2 in 1950 to 63.9 in 1985 (Stonich, 1986:145). Popu-

TABLE 4 Population Density, Number of Years of Fallow, and Ratio of Length of Cropping Cycle to Total Cycle[a], 1950 to 1990

	Period			
Characteristics	1950	Mid-1970s	Mid-1980s	1990
Western and eastern highlands				
Population density (inhab./km^2)	63	99	110	130
Years of fallow	3 to 5	0 to 2	0	0
Ratio[b]	.38 to .6	.6 to 1	1	1
Central highlands				
Population density (inhab./km^2)	35	54	68	74
Years of fallow	15 to 20	10 to 15	2 to 6	0 to 3
Ratio	.13 to .16	.16 to .23	.38 to .6	.6 to 1

[a]Total cycle = years of cultivation plus years of fallow.
[b]The number of years the land is cultivated divided by the number of years the land is fallow.

SOURCE: Stonich (1990).

lation densities are as high as 160 persons/km^2 in some counties (Stonich, 1989:277). Although the natality rate is higher than the national average, growth rates have not kept pace with the rest of the nation—due in part to an infant mortality rate that is 20 percent higher than the national average and in part to regional outmigration. In our research communities, the high regional natality rate is dramatically manifested. The community surveys record an average of 6.3 live births per woman, and many women had yet to complete their families.

Table 4 shows the relationship over time between the increasing population density of highland communities and the number of years the land was allowed to remain fallow. Since 1950, the amount of time fields have been allowed to remain fallow has declined precipitously (Stonich, 1986; Boyer, 1983).[14] As the population density of these highland communities has increased, there has been a corresponding increase in the intensity of land use. Yet simultaneous population increase is not a *sufficient* causal explanation for the intensity of land use, destruction of forests, soil erosion, or other ecological problems of the region. Inequality in access to land and the investment patterns of large landowners, neither of which depend on

---

[14]Although Durham (1979) and DeWalt and DeWalt (1982) do not include comparable quantitative data on this point, their anecdotal evidence indicates a similar pattern.

population pressure, are much more important factors. As we have shown, the expansion of livestock and other commercial agricultural concerns has: (1) created ecological problems because of the heavy use of pesticides, destruction of mangroves in coastal areas, and the mining of land resources; (2) resulted in a continuing decrease in wage-labor opportunities in the region; and (3) removed the poor from access to the better lands; the displaced poor, in turn, have caused ecological problems through the overuse of steep hillside lands on which they are forced to eke out a living.

Although the ecological consequences of commercial agricultural expansion are quite pronounced, it must be emphasized that the social consequences are even more serious. Rural unemployment averaged 62.2 percent over the annual cropping cycle in 1980 (CONSUPLANE, 1982); this figure underestimates unemployment, as women were not included. Since 1980, decreasing cotton and coffee production in the region has further limited agricultural employment opportunities. The result is that many households are unable to satisfy their most basic needs. The national planning agency (SAPLAN, 1981) estimated that 41 percent of all southern families did not meet minimum subsistence levels, and that families living in "semiurban communities" consumed even fewer calories than rural families (Stonich, 1986:152-154).[15]

Data that we collected in 1982 in nine highland and lowland communities showed that 65 percent of the children under 60 months of age were stunted (below 95 percent of the standard height-for-age recommended by the World Health Organization) and 14 percent were wasted (below 90 percent of the standard weight-for-height). Furthermore, in a region in which cattle production is so pervasive, only 3 percent of all the protein consumed by these villagers comes from meat. While most families had access to sufficient protein, half failed to meet energy requirements in some communities (DeWalt and DeWalt, 1987:39). Infant mortality averaged 99/1,000, and an average of 16 percent of all children born in the communities did not survive beyond the age of five. Both undernutrition and child mortality are directly related to the inability of farm families to gain access to enough land to sustain themselves (DeWalt and DeWalt, 1982, 1989; Durham, 1979).

When families cannot survive on the land, they seek opportunities elsewhere (Durham, 1979). Thus, the problems plaguing the south are being exported to other regions of the country. Poor families increasingly engage

---

[15]Average nutritional levels, for example, were lower in the late 1980s than in 1970; the average energy deficit in rural areas was approximately 20 percent (USAID, 1989a); and 38 percent of Honduran children under the age of five exhibited some degree of malnutrition (SAEH/INCAP, 1987).

in cyclical or permanent migration to the cities or depend on remittances from family members. Since 1974, out-migration from the Southern region has averaged 1.3 percent annually. Approximately half as many people leave the region permanently every year as are added to the population by both its high birth rate and in-migration. In the communities we have studied, 70 percent of male household heads and 20 percent of female household heads in Cacautare had migrated at least once to work outside the community. In villages around Esquimay, 39 percent of children over 13 years of age had migrated. Most of these migrants end up in the cities of Honduras.

The urban population growth rate in Honduras was 5.8 percent between 1974 and 1980, and 5.4 percent between 1980 and 1987, a rate much higher than the population growth rate of about 3.5 percent (USAID, 1989a). The squalid slums on the edges of Tegucigalpa and San Pedro Sula attest to the environmental problems caused by this rural-to-urban migration.

Migrants from degraded areas in the south are also settling in Olancho and the vast, relatively unpopulated areas of the Mosquitia in northeastern Honduras—including the Rio Platano Biosphere Reserve. Similar to processes occurring in other areas of Latin America, deforestation has taken a heavy toll on the ecosystems as newly arriving colonizers clear forest for crops, cattle, and fuelwood. The cleared lands often end up in the hands of extensive cattle ranching interests as the colonists move further into the forest, simultaneously encroaching upon lands inhabited by the small remaining indigenous population.

The consequences of land concentration and the expansion of environmentally costly commercial agriculture have been most severe for those who are powerless to alter the course of these events, but the economic and environmental sustenance of all of Honduran society is threatened by these processes.

CONCLUSION

The implications of this case study are clear: A decline in population growth will not have a major impact on slowing the rate of natural resource destruction in Honduras. In southern Honduras, environmental degradation and social problems often attributed to population pressure arise from glaring inequalities in the distribution of land, the lack of decent employment opportunities, and the stark poverty of many of the inhabitants. It is not the carrying capacity of the land that has failed to keep pace with population growth. Neither is population growth the primary cause of the impoverishment of the Honduran ecology and its human inhabitants. While the destruction caused by the poor in their desperate search for survival is alarming, it pales in comparison with the destruction wrought by large landowners through their reckless search for profit.

REFERENCES

Boyer, Jefferson
    1983   Agrarian Capitalism and Peasant Praxis in Southern Honduras. Unpublished Ph.D. dissertation, University of Michigan, Ann Arbor.

CONSUPLANE (Secretaria Técnica del Consejo Superior de Planificación Económica)
    1982   *Las Regiones: Planificación.* Tegucigalpa, Honduras: CONSUPLANE.

CSPE/OEA (Secretaria Técnica del Consejo Superior de Planificacón Económica y Secretaria General de la Organización de Estados Americanos)
    1982   *Proyecto de Desarrollo Local del Sur de Honduras.* Tegucigalpa, Honduras: CSPE\OEAO.

DeWalt, B.R.
    1983   The cattle are eating the forest. *Bulletin of the Atomic Scientists* 39:18-23.
    1985   Microcosmic and macrocosmic processes of agrarian change in southern Honduras: the cattle are eating the forest. Pp. 165-186 in B.R. DeWalt and P.J. Pelto, eds., *Micro and Macro Levels of Analysis in Anthropology Issues in Theory and Research.* Boulder, Colo.: Westview Press.
    1986   Economic assistance in Central America: development or impoverishment? *Cultural Survival Quarterly* 10:14-18.

DeWalt, B.R., and P. Bidegaray
    1991   The agrarian bases of conflict in Central America. Pp. 19-32 in K. Coleman and G. Herring, eds., *Understanding the Central American Crisis: Sources of Conflict, U.S. Policy, and Options for Peace.* Wilmington, Del.: SR Books.

DeWalt, B.R., and K.M. DeWalt
    1982   *Cropping Systems in Pespire, Southern Honduras.* Farming Systems Research in Southern Honduras Report No. 1. Lexington: Department of Anthropology, University of Kentucky.

DeWalt, K.M., and B.R. DeWalt
    1987   Nutrition and agricultural change in southern Honduras. *Food and Nutrition Bulletin* 9(3):36-45.
    1989   Incorporating nutrition into agricultural research: a case study from southern Honduras. Pp. 179-199 in J. van Willigen, B. Rylko-Bauer, and A. McElroy, eds., *Making Our Research Useful: Case Studies in the Utilization of Anthropological Knowledge.* Boulder, Colo.: Westview Press.

DGECH (Dirección General de Estadística y Censos)
    1954   *Censo Nacional Agropecuario 1952.* Tegucigalpa, Honduras: Dirección General de Estadística y Censos.
    1968   *Censo Nacional Agropecuario 1965.* Tegucigalpa, Honduras: Dirección General de Estadística y Censos.
    1976   *Censo Nacional Agropecuario 1974.* Tegucigalpa, Honduras: Dirección General de Estadística y Censos.

Durham, W.
    1979   *Scarcity and Survival in Central America: Ecological Origins of the Soccer War.* Stanford, Calif.: Stanford University Press.

Gonzalez, J.R., D. de Maradiaga, and M.A. Perdomo
    1987   *Situación de la Carcinocultura en la Costa Sur de Honduras.* Tegucigalpa, Honduras: RENARE (cited in SECPLAN/DESFIL, 1989).

Guess, G.M.
    1979   Pasture expansion, forestry, and development contradictions: the case of Costa Rica. *Studies in Comparative International Development* 14:42-55.

Jarvis, L.S.
    1986   *Livestock Development in Latin America.* Washington, D.C.: World Bank.

LACR (Latin American Commodities Report)
  1989 Shrimp/Ecuador. *Latin American Commodities Report.* CR-89-09(15 September):8. London: Latin American Newsletters Ltd.
Leonard, H.J.
  1987 *Natural Resources and Economic Development in Central America.* New Brunswick, N.J.: Transaction Books.
Meckenstock, D., D. Coddington, J. Rosas, H. van Es, M. Chinman, and M. Murillo
  1991 Honduras Concept Paper: Towards a Sustainable Agriculture in Southern Honduras. Paper presented at the International Sorghum/Millet Collaborative Research Support Conference, Corpus Christi, Texas, July 8-12.
Parsons, J.J.
  1976 Forest to pasture: development or destruction? *Revista de Biologia Tropical* 24(Suppl. 1):121-38.
SAEH/INCAP (Servicio de Alimentación Escolar de Honduras/ Instituto de Nutrición de Centro América y Panamá)
  1987 *Primer Censo Nacional de Talla en Escolares de Primer Grado de Educación Primaria de la República de Honduras, 1986.* Tegucigalpa, Honduras: SAEH/INCAP.
SAPLAN (Sistema de Análisis y Planificación de Alimentación y Nutrición)
  1981 *Análisis de la Situación Nutricional durante el Periodo 1972-1979.* Mimeograph. Consejo Superior de Planificación Económico, Tegucigalpa, Honduras.
SECPLAN (Secretaria de Planificación, Coordinación, y Presupuesto) and DESFIL (Development Strategies for Fragile Lands)
  1989 *Perfil Ambiental de Honduras 1989.* Tegucigalpa, Honduras: SECPLAN.
Sheahan, J.
  1987 *Patterns of Development in Latin America.* Princeton, N.J.: Princeton University Press.
Stares, R.C.
  1972 *La Economia Campesina en la Zona Sur de Honduras, 1950-1970: Su Desarrollo y Perspectivas para el Futuro.* Informe Presentado a la Prefectura de Choluteca, Honduras.
Stonich, S.C.
  1986 Development and Destruction: Interrelated Ecological, Socioeconomic, and Nutritional Change in Southern Honduras. Unpublished PhD dissertation, University of Michigan, Ann Arbor.
  1989 The dynamics of social processes and environmental destruction: a Central American case study. *Population and Development Review* 15:269-296.
  1990 Strategies to Enhance Household Agricultural Production and Rehabilitate Degraded Lands in Honduras. Paper presented at the 89th Annual Meeting of the American Anthropological Association, New Orleans, Louisiana, November 30.
  In Press *Enduring Crises: The Political Ecology of Poverty and Environmental Destruction in Honduras.* Boulder, Colo.: Westview Press.
Stonich, S.C. and B.R. DeWalt
  1989 The political economy of agricultural growth and rural transformation in Honduras and Mexico. Pp. 202-230 in S. Smith and E. Reeves, eds., *Human Systems Ecology: Studies in the Integration of Political Economy, Adaptation, and Socionatural Regions.* Boulder, Colo.: Westview Press.
Teller, C., R. Sibrian, C. Talavera, V. Bent, J. del Canto, and L. Saenz
  1979 Population and nutrition: implications of socio-demographic trends and differentials for food and nutrition policy in Central America and Panama. *Ecology of Food and Nutrition* 8:95-109.

USAID (United States Agency for International Development)
   1982   *Country Environmental Profile.* Rosslyn, Va.: JRB Associates.
   1985   *Environmental Assessment of the Small Scale Shrimp Farming Component of the USAID/Honduras Rural Technologies Project.* Gainesville, Fla.: Tropical Research and Development, Inc.

USAID Honduras
   1989a   Strategic Considerations for the Agricultural Sector in Honduras. Draft report. Office of Agriculture and Rural Development, USAID/Honduras, Tegucigalpa.
   1989b   *Plan de Desarrollo del Camarón en Honduras.* Tegucigalpa, Honduras: USAID.
   1990   *Agricultural Sector Strategy Paper.* Tegucigalpa, Honduras: USAID Office of Agriculture and Rural Development.

White, R.A.
   1977   Structural Factors in Rural Development: The Church and the Peasant in Honduras. Unpublished PhD dissertation, Cornell University.

Williams, R.G.
   1986   *Export Agriculture and the Crisis in Central America.* Chapel Hill: University of North Carolina Press.

World Bank
   1991   *World Tables, 1991.* Baltimore: Johns Hopkins University Press.

9
Population Growth, Environmental Change, and Innovation: Implications for Sustainable Growth in Agriculture

Vernon W. Ruttan

In this paper I explore a number of agricultural, resource, and environmental concerns that will condition the capacity of the agricultural sector to respond to the demands that population and income growth will place on the sector—particularly in the developing countries of Latin America, Asia, and Africa.

CONCERNS ABOUT RESOURCES AND THE ENVIRONMENT

I first place these concerns about the implications of natural resource availability and environmental change within a broader historical and theoretical context. We are now in the midst of the third wave of social concern since World War II about the implications of natural resource availability and environmental change for the sustainability of improvements in human well-being.

The Three Waves of Concern

The *first* wave of concern, in the late 1940s and early 1950s, focused primarily on the quantitative relationships between resource availability and economic growth—the adequacy of land, water, energy, and other natural resources to sustain growth. The reports of the President's Water Resources Policy Commission (1950) and the President's Materials Policy Commission (1952) were the landmarks of the early postwar resource assessment studies generated in response to this wave of concern. The primary response to this first wave of concern was technical change. In retrospect it appears that a stretch of high prices has not yet failed to induce the new knowledge and new technologies needed to locate new deposits of natural resources, promote substitution, and enhance productivity. If the Materials Policy Commission were writing today, it would have to conclude that there has been abundant evidence of the nonevident becoming evident; the expensive cheap; and the inaccessible accessible (Barnett and Morse, 1963; Ausubel and Sladovich, 1989).

The *second* wave of concern occurred in the late 1960s and early 1970s. The earlier concern with the potential "limits to growth" imposed by natural resource scarcity was supplemented by concern about the capacity of the environment to assimilate the multiple forms of pollution generated by growth. An intense conflict was emerging between the two major sources of demand for environmental services. One was the rising demand for environmental assimilations of residuals derived from growth in commodity production and consumption—asbestos in our insulation, pesticides in our food, smog in the air, and radioactive wastes in the biosphere. The second was the rapid growth in consumer demand for environmental amenities—for direct consumption of environmental services—arising out of rapid growth in per capita income and high-income elasticity of demand for such environmental services as access to natural environments and freedom from pollution and congestion (Ruttan, 1971). The response to these concerns, still incomplete, was the creation of local and regional institutions designed to force individual firms and other organizations to bear the costs arising from the externalities generated by commodity production.

Since the mid-1980s these two earlier concerns have been supplemented by a *third*. These newer concerns center around the implications for environmental quality, food production, and human health of a series of environmental changes that are occurring on a transnational scale—issues such as global warming, ozone depletion, acid rain, and others (National Research Council, 1990, 1991). The institutional innovations needed to respond to these concerns will be more difficult to design. They will, like the sources of change, need to be transnational or international. Experience with attempts to design incentive-compatible transnational regimes, such as the Law of the Sea Convention, or even the somewhat more successful Montreal Protocol on reduction of CFC emissions, suggests that the difficulty of resolving free rider and distributional equity issues imposes a severe constraint on how rapidly effective transnational regimes to overcome these new environmental concerns can be put in place.

It is of interest that, with each new wave of concern, the issues that dominated the earlier wave were recycled. The result is that while the intensity of earlier concerns has receded, in part due to the induced technical and institutional changes, the concerns about the relationships between resource and environmental change and sustainable growth in agricultural production has broadened (Graham-Tomasi, 1991). Terms that had initially been introduced by the populist critics of agricultural research—such as alternative, low-input, regenerative, and sustainable agriculture—began to enter the vocabulary of those responsible for agricultural research resource allocation.

The Agricultural Transformation

In the closing years of the twentieth century we are completing one of the most remarkable transitions in the history of agriculture. Prior to this century almost all the increase in food production was obtained by bringing new land into production. There were only a few exceptions to this generalization—in limited areas of East Asia, the Middle East, and Western Europe (Hayami and Ruttan, 1985).

By the first decade of the next century, almost all of the increases in world food production must come from higher yields—from increased output per hectare. In most of the world the transition from a resource-based to a science-based system of agriculture is occurring within a single century. Most of the countries of the developing world have been caught up in the transition only since midcentury. Among developing countries those countries of East, Southeast, and South Asia have proceeded further in this transition than have most countries in Latin America or Africa.

Recent historical trends in production and consumption of the major food grains could easily be taken as evidence that one should not be excessively concerned about the capacity of the world's farmers to meet future food demands. World wheat prices, corrected for inflation, have declined since the middle of the last century. Rice prices have declined since the middle of this century (Edwards, 1988; Pingali, 1988). These trends suggest that productivity growth has been able to more than compensate for the rapid growth in demand, particularly during the decades since World War II.

As we look toward the future, however, the sources of productivity growth are not as apparent as they were a quarter century ago. The demands that the developing economies will place on their agricultural producers from population growth and growth in per capita consumption arising out of higher income will be exceedingly high. Population growth rates are expected to decline substantially in most countries during the first quarter of the next century. But the absolute increases in population size will be large and increases in per capita incomes will add substantially to food demand. The effect of growth in per capita income will be more rapid growth in demand for animal proteins and for maize and other feed crops. During the next several decades growth in food and feed demand rising from growth in population and income will run upwards of 4.0 percent per year in many countries. Many will experience more than a doubling of food demand before the end of the second decade of the next century.

CHANGES INDUCED BY POPULATION GROWTH[1]

In the theory of induced innovation, changes in relative resource endowments, such as shifts in the ratio of agricultural labor to land, are viewed as directing technical change along a path that permits the substitution of relatively more abundant factors for the relatively scarce factors of production. Institutional changes are also viewed as induced by changes in relative resource endowments, by changes in cultural endowments, and by changes in technology.

Induced Technical Change[2]

The process by which technical change is generated has traditionally been treated as exogenous to the economic system—as a product of autonomous advances in scientific and technical knowledge. Over the last several decades, advances in economic theory and the accumulation of empirical evidence have tended to confirm that the rate and direction of technical change can be interpreted as largely endogenous to the economic system— as induced by differences or changes in the conditions of factor supply and product demand. In agriculture, the constraints imposed on development by an inelastic supply of land may be offset by advances in biological technology; the constraints imposed by an inelastic supply of labor may be offset by advances in mechanical technology.

In the dynamic process of economic development, changes in product demand and relative factor prices are inseparably related. For example, when food demand rises because of growth in population or per capita income, or both, the demand for factor inputs in food production increases more or less proportionally. When increases in factor demands are confronted with different elasticities in the supply of production factors, the effect is a change in relative factor prices. The different rates of change in factor prices result, in turn, in changes in the level of income and income distribution among factor owners, thereby affecting the aggregate product demand.

---

[1]This section draws on two earlier papers in which Yujiro Hayami and I have used the induced innovation framework to explore the relationships among resource endowments, population change, and technical change (Hayami and Ruttan, 1987, 1991). Our work on induced technical change was first outlined in Hayami and Ruttan (1971). The concept of induced institutional innovation was developed more fully in Binswanger and Ruttan (1978), Hayami and Kikuchi (1981), Ruttan and Hayami (1984), and Hayami and Ruttan (1985).

[2]The history of thought and current state of knowledge in the field of induced technical change is reviewed by Thirtle and Ruttan (1987).

The significance of the induced technical change hypothesis for economic development is that multiple paths of technical change are available to society. The ability of a society to achieve rapid growth in agricultural productivity and output seems to hinge on its ability to make efficient choices among alternative paths. There is substantial evidence that the direction of technical changes has been responsive to relative resource endowments in both the agricultural and nonagricultural sectors, in both traditional and modern societies (Thirtle and Ruttan, 1987).

The initial tests of the induced-innovation hypothesis were against the experience of the United States and Japan for the period 1880-1960. Additional tests have been conducted against the experience of other developed and developing countries. The Japan-U.S. tests have now been extended from 1880-1960 to 1880-1980 (Hayami and Ruttan, 1985). In 1880, Japan and the United States were characterized by extreme differences in relative endowments of land and labor. These differences have widened over time. By 1980, total agricultural land area per male worker was more than 100 times as large and arable land area per male worker about 50 times as large in the United States as in Japan.

The relative prices of land and labor also differed sharply in the two countries. In 1880, to buy a hectare of arable land, a Japanese hired farm worker would have had to work 8 times as many days as a U.S. farm worker. By 1960, a Japanese farm worker would have had to work 30 times as many days as a U.S. farm worker to buy one hectare of arable land. This gap was reduced after 1960, partly because of extremely rapid increases in wage rates in Japan. In the United States, land prices rose sharply in the postwar period. Yet in 1980, a Japanese farm worker still would have had to work 11 times as many days as a U.S. worker to buy one hectare of land.

The relationships between relative factor prices and factor use portrayed in Figures 1.A and 1.B are clearly consistent with the hypothesis that the alternative paths of technical change followed by Japan and the United States have been induced by relative resource endowments interpreted through relative factor prices. When simple relationships emerge as powerfully as they do in Figures 1.A and 1.B, one is tempted to forego more formal tests. The intuitive implications of the data presented in these two figures have, however, been confirmed by more formal tests.[3]

The question is frequently raised as to whether advances in indigenous

---

[3] A method for measuring biases of technical change with many factors of production was originally developed by Hans Binswanger (1974, 1978) using the transcendental logarithmic (translog) function. In our 1985 study, Hayami and I employed a two-level constant elasticity of substitution (CES) production function (Hayami and Ruttan, 1985, 1987). The results of the 1985 study were confirmed by Kawagoe et al. (1986) using a more general model. The Binswanger method was applied to Japanese agriculture by Kako (1978) and Nghiep (1979).

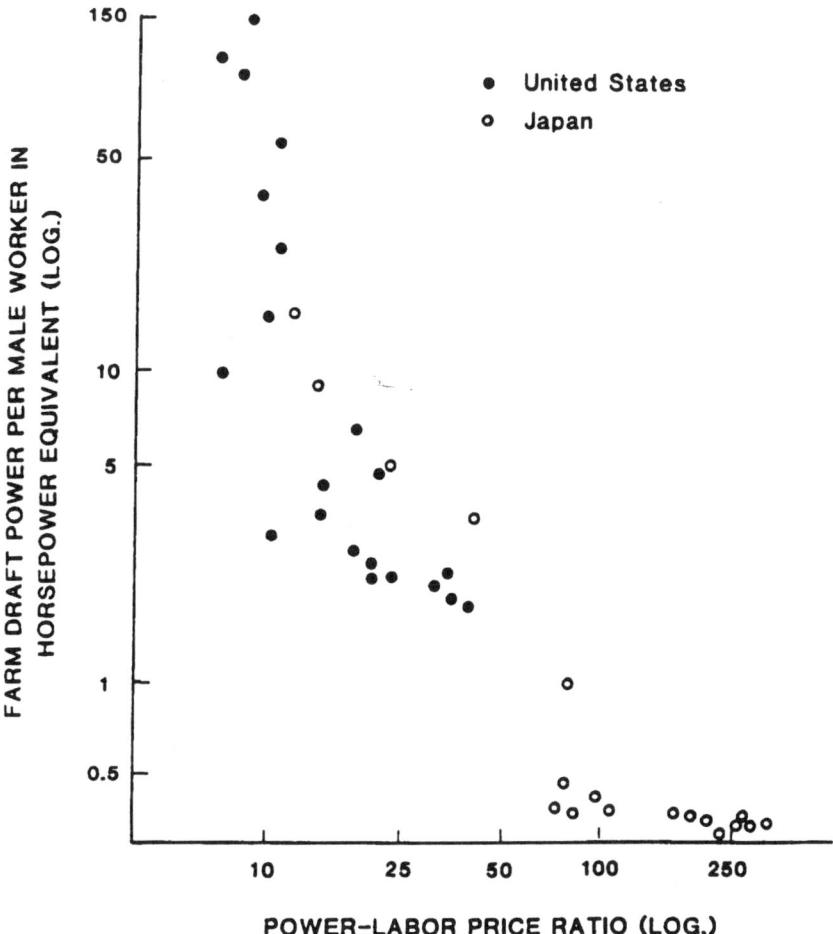

FIGURE 1.A Relationship between farm draft power per male worker and power-labor price ratio, the United States and Japan: quinquennial observations for 1880-1980. NOTE: Equals number of workdays that can be purchased by one horsepower of tractor or draft animal. SOURCE: Hayami and Ruttan (1985). Reprinted with permission.

technology induced by population density, along the lines outlined by Boserup (1965) and more recently by Binswanger and several colleagues (Pingali et al., 1987) would be sufficient to sustain rising levels of per capita income and consumption (Robinson and Schutjer, 1984). A positive response would be excessively romantic. We agree with Boserup that in preindustrial societies, agricultural production often responded "far more generously to addi-

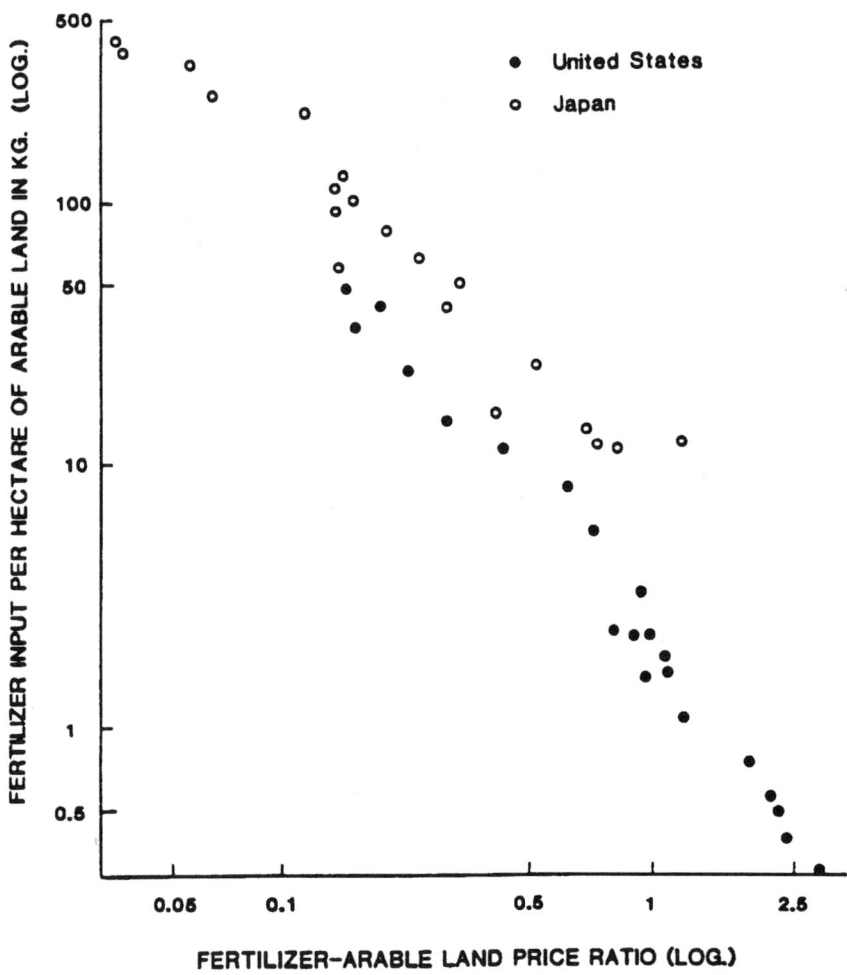

FIGURE 1.B Relationship between fertilizer input per hectare of arable and the fertilizer-arable land price ratio, the United States and Japan: quinquennial observations for 1880-1980. NOTE: Equals hectares of arable land that can be purchased by one ton of N + P_2O_t + K_2O contained in commercial fertilizers. SOURCE: Hayami and Ruttan (1985). Reprinted with permission.

tional inputs of labor than assumed by Neo-Malthusian authors" (Boserup, 1965:15). But Boserup herself argued that the transition to more intensive cultivation would be accompanied by a rise in the number of days worked per year and a decline in output per hour worked (1965:30). And we should not ignore the findings of Ronald Lee that in preindustrial England, annual population growth rates beyond 0.4 percent had "dramatic consequences." The effect of more rapid population growth rates was to raise rents and turn the domestic terms of trade against the agricultural sector (Lee, 1980:547).[4] Under preindustrial conditions, growth in output per hectare was typically accompanied by reductions in output per unit of labor input. However, a decline in labor productivity, measured in terms of output per hour or per day, if accompanied by an increase in the number of hours or days worked per year, is not incompatible with a rise in annual output or income per worker. This is the classic pattern followed on the wet rice cultivation areas of East Asia during the shift from upland to rainfed rice production, and then from rainfed to irrigated rice production. It is the pattern described by Binswanger and his colleagues in the transition in farming systems and technology from forest fallow to multiple cropping. In the long run, however, even with relatively slow growth in population or labor force, output per worker per year tends to stagnate or decline as the response of indigenous technical change to population growth declines.

The higher rates of growth in agricultural production, and in output per hectare and per worker, that are consistent with modern population and income growth rates, have required institutionalization of capacity to supplement indigenous knowledge with science-based knowledge and craft-generated technology with industrial inputs that embody advances in scientific and technical knowledge. It also requires institutionalization of the capacity to deliver the new knowledge and the new technology to farm people and higher levels of investment in human capital in rural areas if the new technical opportunities are to be effectively exploited.

Induced Institutional Change

In the previous section, a model was outlined in which technical change was treated as largely endogenous to the economic system. But the success of the theory of induced technical change gives rise to the need for a more adequate understanding of the sources of institutional change. Institutions are the rules of society, or of organizations, that facilitate coordination among people by helping them form expectations that each person can reasonably hold in dealing with others. They reflect the conventions that have evolved in different societies regarding the behavior of individuals and groups relative to their own behavior and the behavior of others. In the area of economic relations, they have a crucial role in establishing expectations about the rights to use resources in economic activities and about the parti-

---

[4]There is not, however, complete consensus on Lee's results; see Weir (1991).

tioning of the income streams resulting from economic activity (Runge, 1981a:xvi, 1981b; Sen, 1967).[5]

The sources of *demand* for technical and institutional change can be viewed as being essentially similar. A rise in the price of land (or natural resources) in relation to the price of labor induces technical changes that release the constraints on production from an inelastic supply of land, and, at the same time, induces institutional change that leads to greater precision in the definition and allocation of property rights in land. A rise in the price of labor relative to land (or natural resources) induces technical changes that permit the substitution of capital for labor and at the same time induces institutional changes that enhance the productivity of the human agent and increase workers' control over the conditions of employment. The new income streams generated by technical change and by institutional efficiency induce changes in the relative demand for products and open up new and more profitable opportunities for product innovations.

Shifts in the *supply* of technical and institutional change may also be generated by similar forces. Advances in knowledge in science and technology reduce the cost of the new income streams that are generated by technical change. Advances in knowledge in the social sciences and related professions reduce the cost of the new income streams that are generated by gains in institutional innovation and improvements in institutional performance. Collective action leading to changes in the supply of institutional innovations often involves severe stress among the interest groups and communities that stand to gain or lose from the changes. The rate and direction of institutional change depends critically on cultural traditions and ideology that influence the cost or acceptability of changes in institutional arrangements and on the power balance among interest groups. Education, both general and technical, that facilitates a better understanding among people of their common interests can reduce the cost of institutional innovation.

We illustrate, in Figure 2, the elements of a model that maps the general equilibrium relationships among resource endowments, cultural endowments, technologies, and institutions. The model goes beyond the conven-

---

[5]There is considerable disagreement regarding the meaning of the term *institution*. A distinction is often made between the concepts of institution and organization. The broad view that includes both concepts is most useful for our purpose and is consistent with the view expressed by both Commons (1950) and Knight (1952). Our definition also encompasses the classification employed by Davis and North (1971:8-9). We employ the more inclusive definition so as to be able to consider changes in the rules or conventions that govern behavior (a) within economic units such as families, firms, and bureaucracies; (b) among economic units, as in the cases of the rules that govern market relationships; and (c) between economic units, as in the case of the relationship between a firm and a regulatory agency.

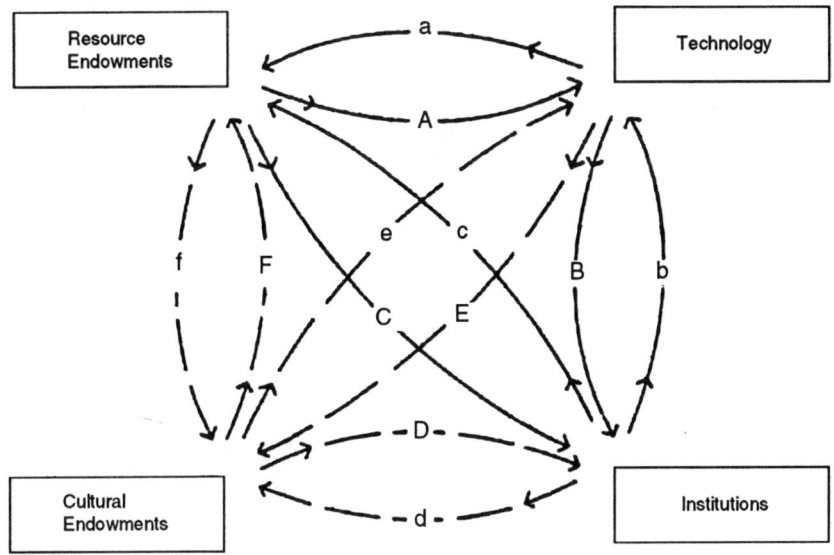

FIGURE 2 Interrelationships between changes in resource endowments, cultural endowments, technology, and institutions. SOURCE: Hayami and Ruttan (1985). Reprinted with permission.

tional general equilibrium model in which resource endowments, technologies, institutions, and culture (conventionally designated as tastes) are given.[6] In the study of long-term social and economic change, the relationships among the several variables must be treated as recursive. The formal microeconomic models that are employed to analyze the supply and demand for technical and institutional change can be thought of as "nested" within the general equilibrium framework of Figure 2.

One advantage of the "pattern model" outlined in Figure 2 is that it helps to identify areas of ignorance. Our capacity to model and test the relationships between resource endowments and technical change is relatively strong. Our capacity to model and test the relationships between cultural endowments and either technical or institutional change is relatively weak. A second advantage of the model is that it is useful in identifying the components that enter into other attempts to account for secular

---

[6]In economics the concept of cultural endowments is usually subsumed under the concept of tastes, which are regarded as given, that is, not subject to economic analysis. Our use of the term *culture* is consistent with the definition suggested by White: "When things and events are considered in the context of their relation to the human organism, they constitute behavior,

economic and social change. Failure to analyze historical change in a general equilibrium context tends to result in a unidimensional perspective on the relationships bearing on technical and institutional change.

For example, historians working within the Marxist tradition often tend to view technical change as dominating both institutional and cultural change. In his book *Oriental Despotism*, Karl Wittfogel views the irrigation technology used in wet rice cultivation in East Asia as determining as political organization (Wittfogel, 1957). As applied to Figure 2, his primary emphasis was on the impact of resources and technology on institutions (B) and (C). A serious misunderstanding can be observed in neo-Marxian critiques of the green revolution. These criticisms have focused attention almost entirely on the impact of technical change on labor and land tenure relations. Both the radical and populist critics have emphasized relation (B). But they have tended to ignore relationships (A) and (C). This bias has led to repeated failure to identify effectively the separate effects of population growth and technical change on the growth and distribution of income (Cleaver, 1972; Griffin, 1974).

Armen Alchian and Harold Demsetz identify a primary function of property rights as guiding incentives to achieve greater internalization of externalities (Alchian and Demsetz, 1973; Demsetz, 1967). They consider that the clear specifications of property rights reduces transaction costs in the face of growing competition for the use of scarce resources as a result of population growth and/or growth in production demand. North and Thomas (1970), building on the Alchian-Demsetz paradigm, attempted to explain the economic growth of western Europe between 900 and 1700 primarily in terms of changes in property institutions.[7] During the eleventh and thirteenth centuries the pressure of population against increasingly scarce land resources induced innovations in property rights that in turn created profitable opportunities for the generation and adoption of labor-intensive technical changes in agriculture (line C).

In a more recent work, Mancur Olson has emphasized the proliferation of institutions as a source of economic decline (Olson, 1982).[8] He also

---

when they are considered . . . in their relationship to one another, they become culture" (1974:1152). We use the term *cultural endowments* to capture those dimensions of culture that have been transmitted from the past. Contemporary changes in resource endowments, technology, and institutions can be expected to result in changes in cultural endowments. For a discussion of attempts to employ the concept of culture by development economists, see Ruttan (1988a).

[7] For a critical review of the North-Thomas model, see Field (1981). Field is critical of attempts by North and Thomas to treat institutional change as endogenous. For criticism of the Hayami-Ruttan approach to induced institutional change, see Koppel and Oasa (1987); Burmeister (1987); and Bromley (1989).

[8] For a critical review of the Olson work, see North (1983).

regards broad-based encompassing organizations as having incentives to generate growth and redistribute incomes to their members with little excess burden. For example, a broadly based coalition that encompasses the majority of agricultural producers is more likely to exert political pressure for growth-oriented policies that will enable its members to obtain a larger share of a larger national product than a smaller organization that represents the interests of the producers of a single commodity. But large groups, in Olson's view, are inherently unstable because rational individuals will not incur the costs of contributing to the realization of a large group program— they have strong incentives to act as free riders. As a result, organizational "space" in a stable society will be increasingly occupied by special interest "distributional coalitions." These distributional coalitions make political life divisive. They slow down the adoption of new technologies (line b) and limit the capacity to reallocate resources (line c). The effect is to slow down economic growth or in some cases initiate a period of economic decline.

In some cases the demand for institutional innovation can be satisfied by the development of new forms of property rights, more efficient market institutions, or evolutionary changes arising out of direct contracting by individuals at the level of the community or the firm. In other cases, in which externalities are involved, substantial political resources may have to be brought to bear to organize nonmarket institutions to provide for the supply of public goods.

Research conducted by Hayami and Kikuchi (Kikuchi and Hayami, 1978; Hayami and Kikuchi, 1981) in the Philippines in the late 1970s enables us to examine a contemporary example of the interrelated effects of technical change and population growth on the demand for institutional change in land tenure and labor relations. In the Philippines case they studied, the induced-innovation process leading toward the establishment of equilibrium in factor markets occurred rather rapidly even though many of the transactions—between landlords, tenants, and laborers—were less than fully monetized. Informal contractual arrangements or agreements were used. The subleasing and the *gamma* labor contract evolved without the mobilization of substantial political activity or bureaucratic effort because the contracting parties shared common cultural endowments.

The development and introduction of new institutions in larger populations characterized by considerable cultural heterogeneity would require the mobilization of substantial bureaucratic and political resources. A richer model is needed in environments in which (a) institutional change involves the redistribution of existing resources or income shares rather than the partitioning of growth dividends or (b) inequities in the distribution of economic and political resources preclude the kind of simple recontracting that characterized the Philippine village case of Hayami and Kikuchi.[9] Its value is that it exhibits so clearly the interaction of population pressure, change in agricultural technology, and change in agrarian institutions.

Induced Innovation and the Environment

We are, as noted in the introduction, now in the third post-World War II wave of concern about the implications of natural resource availability and environmental change for the sustainability of improvements in human well-being. Over this period we have seen a transition from primary concern with the material basis for agricultural and industrial development to the impact of the intensification of agricultural and industrial activity on the environment—from a concern about the material basis of production to the "sink" capacity of the environment. One effect of this transition has been to weaken the signals provided by market forces on the rate and direction of technical and institutional change.

Under present institutional arrangements substantial components of the physical and social environments continue to be undervalued for purposes of market transactions, even though they have become common property resources of great and increasing value. The effect has been to bias the rate and direction of technical change toward excessive production of a wide range of residual and spillover effects and away from increased efficiency in the supply of resource amenities (Ruttan, 1971).

In this view the environmental stress resulting from pollution and from the transformation of land use in fragile environments is not simply a by-product of the autonomous forces of population and income growth or of technical change. The system of legal and economic institutions that govern the use of common property resources has failed to evolve in a manner consistent with (a) the rising demand for capacity to receive and assimilate the residuals associated with commodity production and consumption and

---

[9]Boyce (1987) finds that in Bangladesh, where the institutional environment is severely biased by market imperfections and unequal distribution of economic and political resources, that differences in population density and population growth rates influence the rate and direction of technical change in a manner consistent with the induced technical change hypothesis (pp. 138-161). He also finds that these imperfections in economic and political markets have represented a serious constraint on the development and reform of irrigation and other water control institutions (pp. 162-200). The induced-innovation framework outlined and employed in this paper has been referred to by Boyce (pp. 25-30) as the "pure" theory of institutional innovation. In other work, we have drawn on cases, such as those described in the work of de Janvry (1973), Sanders and Ruttan (1978), and Feeny (1982) in which biases in political resources acted to prevent or delay the process of induced institutional innovation and in which substantial political and bureaucratic resources had to be mobilized to transform the latent demand into effective demand for institutional change.

(b) the shift to the right in the demand for resource amenities associated with high and rising per capita incomes.

Traditional production theory implies that if the price of a factor input is zero (or close to zero) that factor will be used until the value of its marginal product approaches zero. This will occur even though the marginal social product may be negative. In an environment characterized by rapid economic growth, technical changes induced by changes in relative factor prices will bias the direction of technical change. The demand for a resource that is priced below its social cost will grow more rapidly than it would in a situation in which substitution possibilities can occur only along a "given" production surface. The effect is to accelerate the widening gap between the private and social costs of environmental services.

The situation in which we find ourselves—in which there is a widening gap between the inducements provided by markets and the shadow prices for resource and environmental amenities—comes at a time when the political resources that will be necessary to bring about the needed institutional innovations have been eroding. The implicit demand for market and nonmarket institutional innovations to deal with the spillover effects of agricultural and industrial intensification is clearly rising. The development of effective market institutions, to achieve more efficient use of water resources for example, will require public intervention in market design. New regulatory regimes will be required when market factors continue to represent a constraint on effective resource use. But we are caught in a "time warp" in which ideological currents are running in a direction that has weakened the capacity for public sector institutional design and information.

CONSTRAINTS ON FUTURE AGRICULTURAL PRODUCTION

In this section I discuss some of the (a) scientific and technical constraints and (b) the resource and environmental constraints that can be expected to impinge on sustainable growth in agricultural production as we move into the early decades of the next century. These constraints were identified in a series of consultations held during 1989 and 1990 with the support of the Rockefeller Foundation (Ruttan, 1989, 1992).

Scientific and Technical Constraints

It seems apparent that the gains in agricultural production required over the next quarter century will be achieved with much greater difficulty than in the immediate past. Difficulty is currently being experienced in raising yield ceilings for the cereal crops that have experienced rapid yield gains in the recent past. The incremental response to increases in fertilizer use has declined. Expansion of irrigated area has become more costly. Maintenance research, the research required to prevent yields from declining, is rising as a share of research effort (Plucknett and Smith, 1986). The institutional capacity to respond to these concerns is limited, even in the countries with the most effective national research and extension systems. Indeed, there has been considerable difficulty in many countries during the 1980s in maintaining the agricultural research capacity that had been established during the 1960s and 1970s (Cummings, 1989).

It is possible that within another decade, advances in basic knowledge will create new opportunities for advancing agricultural technology that will reverse the urgency of some of the above-mentioned concerns. The institutionalization of private sector agricultural research capacity in some developing countries is beginning to complement public sector capacity (Pray, 1983). Advances in molecular biology and genetic engineering are occurring rapidly. But the date when these promising advances will be translated into productive technology seems to be receding. The limits arising out of scientific and technical constraints have important implications for agricultural research agendas.

Advances in conventional technology will remain the primary source of growth in crop and animal production over the next quarter century. Almost all increases in agricultural production over the next several decades must continue to come from further intensification of agricultural production on land that is presently devoted to crop and livestock production. Until well into the second decade of the next century the necessary gains in crop and animal productivity will be generated by improvements from conventional plant and animal breeding and from more intensive and efficient use of technical inputs including chemical fertilizers, pesticides and more effective animal nutrition. The productivity gains from conventional sources are likely to come in smaller increments than in the past. If they are to be realized, higher plant populations per unit area, new tillage practices, improved pest and disease control, more precise application of plant nutrients, and advances in soil and water management will be required. Gains from these sources will be crop, animal, and location specific. They will require closer articulation between the suppliers and users of new knowledge and new technology. These sources of yield gains will be extremely knowledge and information intensive. If they are to be realized, research and technology transfer efforts in the areas of information and management technology must become increasingly important sources of growth in crop and animal productivity.

Advances in conventional technology will be inadequate to sustain the demands that will be placed on agriculture as we move into the second decade of the next century and beyond. Advances in crop yields have come about primarily by increasing the plant populations per hectare and by increasing the ratio of grain to straw in individual plants. Advances in animal feed efficiency have come largely by decreasing the proportion of feed consumed that is devoted to animal maintenance and increasing the proportion used to produce usable animal products. There are severe physiological constraints to continued improvement along these conventional paths. These constraints are most severe in those areas that have already achieved the highest levels of productivity—as in Western Europe, North America, and parts of East Asia. The impact of these constraints can be measured in terms of declining incremental response to energy inputs—both in the form of a reduction in the incremental yield increases from higher levels of fertilizer application, and a reduction in the incremental savings in labor inputs from the use of larger and more powerful mechanical equipment. If the incremental returns to agricultural research should also decline, it will impose a higher priority on efficiency in the organization of research and on the allocation of research resources.

A reorientation of the way we organize agricultural research will be necessary to realize the opportunities for technical change being opened up by advances in microbiology and biochemistry. Advances in basic science, particularly in molecular biology and biochemistry, have and are continuing to open up new possibilities for supplementing traditional sources of plant and animal productivity growth. A wide range of possibilities were discussed at the consultation—ranging from the transfer of growth hormones into fish to conversion of lignocellulose into edible plant and animal products. The realization of these possibilities will require a reorganization of agricultural research systems. An increasing share of the new knowledge generated by research will reach producers in the form of proprietary products or services. This means that incentives must be created to draw substantially more private sector resources into agricultural research. Within the public sector, research will have to move increasingly from a "little science" to a "big science" mode of organization. Examples include the Rockefeller Foundation-sponsored collaborative research program on the biotechnology of rice and the University of Minnesota's program on the biotechnology of maize. In the absence of more focused research efforts, it seems likely that the promised gains in agricultural productivity from biotechnology will continue to recede.

Efforts to institutionalize agricultural research capacity in developing countries must be intensified. Crop and animal productivity levels in most developing countries remain well below the levels that are potentially feasible. Access to the conventional sources of productivity growth—from advances in plant breeding, agronomy, and soil and water management will require the institutionalization of substantial agricultural research capacity for each crop or animal species of economic significance in each agroclimatic region. In a large number of developing countries this capacity is just beginning to be put in place. A number of countries that experienced substantial growth in capacity during the 1960s and 1970s have experienced an erosion of capacity in the 1980s. Even a relatively small country, producing a limited range of commodities under a limited range of agroclimatic conditions, will require a cadre of about 250-300 agricultural scientists. Countries that do not acquire adequate agricultural research capacity will not be able to meet the demands that they will place on their farmers as a result of growth in population and income.

There are substantial possibilities for developing sustainable agricultural production systems in a number of fragile resource areas. Research underway in the tropical rain forest areas of Latin America and in the semiarid tropics of Africa and Asia suggest the possibility of developing sustainable agricultural systems with substantially enhanced productivity even in unfavorable environments. It is unlikely, and perhaps undesirable, that all of these areas should become important components of the global food supply system. But enhanced productivity is important to those who reside in these areas—now and in the future. It is important that the research investment in the areas of soil and water management and in farming systems be intensified in these areas.

There is a need for the establishment of substantial basic biological research and training capacity in the tropical developing countries. There are a series of basic biological research agendas that are important for applied research and technology development for agriculture in the tropics that receive, and are likely to continue to receive, inadequate attention in the temperate region developed countries. There is also a need for closer articulation between training in applied science and technology and training in basic biology. When such institutes are established they will need to be more closely linked with existing academic centers of research and training than the series of agricultural research institutes established by the Rockefeller and Ford Foundations and the Consultative Group on International Agricultural Research.

Resource and Environmental Constraints on Sustainable Growth

As we look even further into the next century, there is a growing concern about the impact of a series of resource and environmental constraints that may seriously impinge on the capacity to sustain growth in agricultural production.

One set of concerns is about the impact of agricultural production practices that will be employed in those areas that have made the most progress in moving toward highly intensive systems of agriculture production. These include loss of soil resources due to erosion, water-logging, and salinization; groundwater contamination from plant nutrients and pesticides; and growing resistance of insects, weeds, and pathogens to present methods of control.

A second set of concerns stem from the impact of industrialization on global climate and other environmental changes (Reilly and Bucklin, 1989; Parry, 1990). There can no longer be much doubt that the accumulation of carbon dioxide (CO_2) and other greenhouse gases—principally methane (CH_4), nitrous oxide (N_2O), and chlorofluorocarbons (CFCs)—has set in motion a process that will result in a rise in global average surface temperatures over the next 30-60 years. The resource and environmental constraints also have important implications for research agendas.

A serious effort to develop alternative land use, farming systems, and food systems scenarios for the twenty-first century should be initiated. A clearer picture of the demands that are likely to be placed on agriculture over the next century and of the ways in which agricultural systems might be able to meet such demands has yet to be produced. Past studies of potential climate change effects on agriculture have given insufficient attention to adaptive change in nonclimate parameters. But application of advances in biological and chemical technology, which substitute knowledge for land, and advances in mechanical and engineering technology, which substitute knowledge for labor, have in the past been driven by increasingly favorable access to energy resources—by declining prices of energy. There will be strong incentive, by the early decades of the next century, to improve energy efficiency in agricultural production and utilization. Particular attention should be given to alternative and competing uses of land. Conversion of low-intensity agricultural systems to forest has been proposed as a method of absorbing CO_2. There will also be increasing demands on land use for watershed protection and biomass energy production.

The capacity to monitor the agricultural sources and impacts of environmental change should be strengthened. It is a matter of serious concern that only in the last decade and a half has it been possible to estimate the magnitude and productivity effects of soil loss even in the United States. Even rudimentary data on productivity effects of soil loss are almost completely unavailable in most developing countries. The same point holds, with even greater force, for groundwater pollution, salinization, species loss, and other topics.

The design of technologies and institutions to achieve more efficient management of surface and groundwater resources will become increasingly important. The development and introduction of technologies and management systems that enhance water use efficiency represents a high priority both because of short- and intermediate-term constraints on water availability and the longer-term possibility of seasonal and geographical shifts in water availability. The identification, breeding, and introduction of water-efficient crops for dryland and saline environments is potentially an important aspect of achieving greater water use efficiency.

Research on environmentally compatible farming systems should be intensified. In agriculture, as in the energy field, a number of technical and institutional innovations could have both economic and environmental benefits. Among the technical possibilities is the design of a new "third-" or "fourth-" generation chemical, biorational, and biological pest management technologies. Another is the design of land use technologies and institutions that will contribute to reduction of erosion, salinization, and groundwater pollution.

Immediate efforts should be made to reform agricultural commodity and income support policies. In both developed and developing countries producers' decisions on land management, farming systems, and use of technical inputs (e.g., fertilizers and pesticides) are influenced by government interventions such as price supports and subsidies, programs to promote or limit production, and tax incentives and penalties. It is increasingly important that such interventions be designed to take into account the environmental consequences of decisions by land owners and producers induced by the interventions.

The agricultural science community should be prepared, by the second quarter of the next century, to contribute to the design of alternative food systems. A food-system perspective should become an organizing principle for improvements in the performance of existing systems and for the design of new systems. Many of these alternatives will include the use of plants other than the grain crops that now account for a major share of world feed and food production. Some of these alternatives will involve radical changes in food sources. Rogoff and Rawlins (1987) have described one such system based on lignocellulose—both for animal feed and human consumption.

A major research program on incentive-compatible institutional design should be initiated. The first research priority is to initiate a large-scale program of research on the design of institutions capable of implementing incentive-compatible resource management policies and programs. By incentive-compatible institutions I mean institutions capable of achieving compatibility between individual, organizational, and social objectives in resource management. A major source of the global warming and environmental pollution problem is the direct result of the operation of institutions which induce behavior by individuals, and public agencies that are not compatible with societal development—some might say survival—goals. In the absence of more efficient incentive compatible institutional design, the transaction costs involved in *ad hoc* approaches are likely to be enormous.

Generic Issues

Many of the problems discussed are international in scope. Many of the institutions that will be needed to enable societies to respond to the constraints on sustainable increases in agricultural production must involve international collaboration or transnational organization.

Our limited capacity to design the institutional infrastructure that will be needed to sustain the required rates of growth in agricultural production as we move through the first decades of the next century must be strengthened. We are going to have to build institutional infrastructures that facilitate more effective collaboration among engineers, agronomists and health scientists—to deal with issues of production, environmental change, and the health of food producers and consumers.

The inadequacy of our capacity to monitor changes in the sources of productivity change, environmental change, and the insults to health must be overcome. We know very little about either the levels or the trajectories of these changes. We talk about soil erosion but we do not have the monitoring capacity to know the extent to which it is weakening our capacity to produce. We are fighting a defensive battle against the health effects of the contamination of our food supply rather than anticipating the sources. One of the puzzling aspects of the data that have become available so far is that the health effects of increased use of fertilizer are less than expected despite high levels of nitrate in surface and groundwater. Neither the developed or developing countries have in place adequate surveillance systems for disease.

SUSTAINABLE GROWTH

In the discussion of the constraints on sustainable growth in agricultural production in the previous section no attempt was made to confront the full implications of the concept of sustainable growth. The concept has emerged as an umbrella under which movements with widely disparate reform agendas have been able to march while avoiding conflicts over their often inconsistent agendas.

Defining Sustainable Growth

Despite the advantages of avoiding defining a term that has apparently been adopted precisely because of its ambiguity, it is useful to trace the evolution of the concept of sustainable growth (Batie, 1989).

Writing in the early 1980s, Gordon K. Douglass identified three alternative conceptual approaches to the definition of agricultural sustainability (Douglass, 1984:3-29). *One group* defined sustainability primarily in technical and economic terms—in terms of the capacity to supply the expanding demand for agricultural commodities on increasingly favorable terms. For this group, primarily mainstream agricultural and resource economists, the long-term decline in the real prices of agricultural commodities was evidence that the growth of agricultural production has been following a sustainable path.

Douglass identified *a second group* that regards agricultural sustainability primarily as an ecological question—"an agricultural system which needlessly depletes, pollutes, or disrupts the ecological balance of natural systems is unsustainable" (Douglass, 1984:2). Among those advancing the ecological sustainability agenda there is a pervasive view that population levels are already too large to be sustained at present levels of per capita consumption (Goodland, 1991).

A third group traveling under the banner of "alternative agriculture" places its primary emphasis on sustaining not just the physical resource base but a broad set of community values (National Research Council, 1989). Its adherents take as a major objective the strengthening or revitalization of rural culture and rural communities guided by a holistic approach to the physical and cultural dimensions of production and consumption.

By the mid-1980s the sustainability concept was diffusing rapidly from the confines of its agroecological origins. The definition that has achieved the widest currency was that adopted by the Bruntland Commission: "Sustainable development is development that meets the needs of the present without compromising the ability of future generations to meet their own needs" (World Commission on Environment and Development, 1987:43). The Bruntland Commission definition raises the possibility that it may be necessary for those of us who are alive today, particularly those of us living in the more affluent societies, to curb our level of material consumption to avoid an even more drastic decline in the consumption levels of future generations. Our historical experience, at least in the West, often causes us to be skeptical about our obligations to future generations. It was less than a generation ago that Robert Solow, one of our leading growth theorists, noted in his Richard T. Ely address to the American Economic Association: "We have actually done quite well at the hands of our ancestors. Given how poor they were and how rich we are, they might properly have saved less and consumed more" (Solow, 1974:9). In most of the world the ancestors have not been so kind!

It is hard to avoid a conclusion that the popularity of the Bruntland Commission definition is due, at least in part, to the fact that the definition is so broad that it is almost devoid of operational significance. The sustainability concept is now undergoing what has been referred to as "establishment appropriation" (Buttel, 1988).

Historically Sustainable Agricultural Systems

We are able to draw on several historical examples of systems that proved capable of meeting the challenge of achieving sustainable increases in agricultural production. One example are the forest and bush fallow (or shifting cultivation) systems practiced in most areas of the world in premodern times and today in many tropical areas (Pingali et al., 1987). At low levels of population density, these systems were sustainable over long periods of time. As population density increased, short fallow systems emerged. Where the shift to short fallow systems occurred slowly, as in Western Europe and East Asia, systems of farming that permitted sustained growth in agricultural production emerged. Where the transition to short fallow has been forced by rapid population growth, the consequence has often been soil degradation and declining productivity.

A second example can be drawn from the agricultural history of East Asian wet rice cultivation (Hayami and Ruttan, 1985). Traditional wet rice cultivation resembled farming in an aquarium. The rice grew tall and rank; it had a low grain-to-straw ratio. Most of what was produced, straw and grain, was recycled in the form of human and animal manures. Mineral nutrients and organic matter were carried into and deposited in the fields with the irrigation water. Rice yields rose continuously, though slowly, even under a monoculture system.

A third example of sustainable agriculture was the system of integrated crop-animal husbandry that emerged in Western Europe in the late middle ages to replace the medieval two- and three-field systems (van Bath, 1963; Boserup, 1965). The "new husbandry" system emerged with the introduction and intensive use of new forage and green manure crops. These in turn permitted an increase in the availability and use of animal manures. This permitted the emergence of intensive crop-livestock systems of production through the recycling of plant nutrients in the form of animal manures to maintain and improve soil fertility.[10]

The three systems that I have described, along with other similar systems based on indigenous technology, have provided an inspiration for the emerging field of agroecology. But none of the traditional systems, while

---

[10]In his study of sustainable agriculture in the middle ages, Jules N. Pretty notes that "Manorial estates survived many centuries of change and appear to have been highly sustainable agricultural systems. Yet this sustainability was not achieved because of high agricultural productivity—indeed it appears that farmers were trading off low productivity against the more highly valued goals of stability, sustainability and equitability. These were promoted by the integrated nature of farming; the great diversity of produce, including wild resources; the diversity of livelihood strategies; the guaranteed source of labor; and the high degree of cooperation" (Pretty, 1990:1).

sustainable under conditions of slow growth in demand, has the capacity to respond to modern rates of growth in demand generated by some combination of rapid increase in population and in growth of income. Some traditional systems were able to sustain rates of growth in the 0.5-1.0 percent per year range. But modern rates of growth in demand are in the range of 1.0-2.0 percent per year in the developed countries. They often rise to the range of 3.0-5.0 percent per year in the less developed and newly industrializing countries. Rates of growth in demand in this range lie outside of the historical experience of the presently developed countries!

In the presently developed countries the capacity to sustain the necessary increases in agricultural production will depend largely on our capacity for institutional innovation. If our capacity to sustain growth in agricultural production is lost, it will be a result of political and economic failures. It is quite clear, however, that the scientific and technical knowledge is not yet available that will enable farmers in most tropical countries to meet the current demand their societies are placing upon them nor to sustain the increases that are currently being achieved. Further, the research capacity has not yet been established that will be necessary to provide the knowledge and the technology needed to sustain and increase farm production. In these countries, achievement of sustainable agricultural surpluses is dependent on advances in scientific knowledge and on technical and institutional innovation (TAC/CGIAR, 1989).

In attempting to design technologies and institutions that are capable of responding to contemporary concerns about sustainability we are confronted with three issues in which our lack of knowledge is fundamental.

The Issue Of Substitutability

One area in which our knowledge is inadequate concerns the role of technology in widening the substitutability among natural resources and between natural resources and reproducible capital. Economists and technologists have traditionally viewed technical change as widening the possibility of substitution among resources—of fertilizer for land, for example (Solow, 1974; Goeller and Weinberg, 1976). The sustainability community rejects the "age of substitutability" argument. The loss of plant genetic resources is viewed as a permanent loss of capacity. The elasticity of substitution among natural factors and between natural and manmade factors is viewed as exceedingly low (James et al., 1989; Daly, 1991). This is an argument, in economists' language, over the form of the production function. While the argument is often cast in philosophical terms, empirical research should lead toward a convergence. If a combination of capital investment and technical change widens the opportunity for substitution, imposing constraints on present resource use could leave subsequent generations less well off. If on the other hand real output per unit of natural resource input is narrowly bounded—i.e., cannot exceed some upper limit that is not too far from where we are now—then catastrophe is unavoidable.

Obligations Toward the Future

The second issue is one that has divided traditional resource economists and the sustainability community. That is the issue of how to deal analytically with the obligations of the present generation toward future generations. The issue of intergenerational equity is at the center of the sustainability debate (Pearce et al., 1990; Solow, 1991). Environmentalists have been particularly critical of the approach used by resource and other economists in valuing future benefit and cost streams. The conventional approach involves the calculation of the "present value" of a resource development or protection project by discounting the cost and benefit stream by some "real" rate of interest—an interest rate adjusted to reflect the costs of inflation. It is World Bank policy (but not always the practice) to require a 10-15 percent rate of return on projects. These higher rates are set well above long-term real rates of interest (historically less than 4 percent) to reflect the effect of unanticipated inflation and other risks associated with project development and implementation. An attempt is made in this way to avoid unproductive projects.

The critics insist that this approach results in a "dictatorship of the present" over the future. At conventional rates of interest the present value of a dollar of benefits 50 years into the future approaches zero. "Discounting can make molehills out of even the biggest mountain" (Batie, 1989:1092). If the marginal profit—marginal revenue less marginal cost—to resource owners rises slower than the rate of interest production is pushed nearer in time and the resource would be exhausted quickly (Solow, 1974:3; Lipton, 1991). As a result of the adoption of a widely held sustainability "ethic," one question has not been adequately answered: would market-determined discount rates decline toward the rate preferred by those advancing the sustainability agenda?[11] Or will it be necessary to impose sumptuary regu-

---

[11] The question of the impact of the use of a positive discount (or interest) rate on resource exploitation decisions is somewhat more complex than is often implied in the sustainability literature. Simply lowering the discount rate to favor the natural resource sector will not assure slower exploitation of natural resources if the market rate of interest remains high. Recipients of the lower interest rates may transfer the revenue from resource exploitation to investments that have higher rates of return rather than reinvesting to sustain the flow of resource benefits. Furthermore, high rates of resource exploitation can be consistent with either high or low interest rates. In the case of forest exploitation, for example, a low discount rate favors letting trees grow longer and the planting of trees that take longer to grow. On the

lations in an effort to induce society to shift the income distribution more strongly toward future generations? It is clear, at least to me, that in most countries efforts to achieve sustainable growth in agricultural production must involve some combination of (a) higher contemporary rates of saving—that is deferring present in favor of future consumption—and (b) more rapid technical change—particularly the technical changes that will enhance resource productivity and widen the range of substitutability among resources.

Incentive Compatible Institutional Design

A third area in which knowledge needs to be advanced is on the design of institutions that are capable of internalizing—within individual households, private firms, and public organizations—the costs of actions that generate the negative spillover effects—the residuals—that are the source of environmental stress. Under present institutional arrangements important elements of the physical and social environment continue to be undervalued for purposes of both market and nonmarket transactions.

The dynamic consequence of failure to internalize these costs are even more severe. In an environment characterized by rapid population and economic growth and changing relative factor prices, failure to internalize resource costs will bias the direction of technical change. The demand for a resource that is priced below its social cost will grow more rapidly than it would in a situation in which substitution possibilities are constrained by existing technology (Ruttan, 1971). As a result "open access" resources will undergo stress or depletion more rapidly than they would in a world characterized by a static technology or even by neutral (unbiased) technical change.

The design of incentive-compatible institutions—institutions capable of achieving compatibility among individual, organizational, and social objectives—remains at this stage an art rather than a science. The incentive-compatibility problem has not been solved even at the most abstract theoretical level.[12] This deficiency in institutional design capacity is evident in

---

other hand, a low discount rate will make it profitable to invest in mineral exploitation, land and water development, or other investment projects that might otherwise be unprofitable. That is why, in the past, resource economists and environmentalists have argued in favor of higher interest rates on public water resource projects (Norgaard, 1991; Price, 1991; Graham-Tomasi, 1991). As an alternative to lower discount rates, Mikesell (1991) suggests taking resource depletion into account in project cost-benefit analysis.

[12]The concept of incentive compatibility was introduced by Hurwicz (1972). In that paper he showed that it was not possible to specify an informationally decentralized mechanism for

our failure to design institutions capable of achieving contemporary distributional equity, either within countries or among rich and poor countries. It impinges with even greater force on our capacity to design institutions capable of achieving intergenerational equity.

AN UNCERTAIN FUTURE

In closing I would like to emphasize how far we are from being able to design either an adequate technological or institutional response to the issue of how to achieve sustainable growth in agricultural production—or in the sustainable growth of both the sustenance and the amenity components of consumption.

At present there is no package of technology available to transfer to producers that can assure the sustainability of growth in agricultural production at a rate that will enable agriculture, particularly in the developing countries, to meet the demands that are being placed on it by rapid growth of population and income. Sustainability is appropriately viewed as a guide to future agricultural research agendas rather than as a guide to practice (Ruttan, 1988b; Graham-Tomasi, 1991). As a guide to research it seems useful to adhere to a definition that would include: (a) the development of technology and practices that maintain and/or advance the quality of land and water resources, and (b) improvement in the performance of plants and animals and advances in production practices that will facilitate the substitution of biological technology for chemical technology. The research agenda on sustainable agriculture needs to explore what is biologically feasible without being excessively limited by present economic constraints.

At present the sustainability community has not been able to advance a program of institutional innovation or reform that can provide a credible guide to the organization of sustainable societies. We have yet to design the institutions that can assure intergenerational equity. Few would challenge the assertion that future generations have rights to levels of sustenance and amenities that are at least equal to those enjoyed (or suffered) by the present generation. They also should expect to inherit improvements in institutional capital—including scientific and cultural knowledge—needed to design more productive and healthy environments.

My conclusion with respect to institutional design is similar to that which I have advanced for technology. Economists and other social scientists have made a good deal of progress in contributing the analysis needed

---

resource allocation that simultaneously generates efficient resource allocation and incentives for consumers to honestly reveal their true preferences. For the current state of knowledge in this area, see Groves et al. (1987).

for "course correction." But capacity to contribute to institutional design remains limited. The fact that the problem of designing incentive-compatible institutions has not been solved at even the most abstract theoretical level means that institutional design proceeds in an ad hoc trial and error basis—and that the errors continue to be expensive. Institutional innovation and reform should represent a high-priority research agenda.

Despite this litany of constraints, my own perspective on agricultural futures is cautiously optimistic. The challenges posed by the constraints on crop and animal productivity and by the resource, environmental, and health constraints on sustainability should not be interpreted as a completely pessimistic assessment. The global agricultural research system, the technology supply industry, and farmers are much better equipped to confront the challenges of the future than they were when confronted with the food crises of the past.

It cannot be emphasized too strongly, however, that the challenges are both technical and institutional. The great institutional innovation of the nineteenth century was "the invention of the method of invention" (Whitehead, 1925:96). The modern industrial research laboratory, the agricultural experiment station, and the research university were a product of this institutional innovation. But it was not until well after midcentury that national and international agricultural research institutions became firmly established in most developing countries. The challenge to institutional innovation in the next century will be to design institutions that can ameliorate the negative spillover into the soil, the water, and the atmosphere of the residuals from agricultural and industrial intensification.

The capacity to achieve sustainable growth in agricultural production and income will also depend on the changes that occur in the economic environment in which farmers in developing countries find themselves. The most favorable economic environment for releasing the constraints on crop and animal productivity and for achieving sustainable adaptation to the resource and environmental constraints that will impinge on agriculture in developing countries is one characterized by slow growth of population and by rapid growth of income and employment in the nonagricultural sector. Failure to achieve sustainable growth in the nonfarm sector could result in farmers in developing countries being able to make adequate food and fiber available to the nonfarm sector only at higher and higher prices—reversing the long-term trend—but with inadequate supplies of the resources needed to generate the investments in resource and technology development necessary to sustain growth.

The importance of favorable growth in the nonfarm economy is particularly important for the landless and near-landless workers in the rainfed upland areas that have been left behind by the advances associated with the seed-fertilizer-water technology of the last quarter century. Rapid growth in demand arising out of higher incomes, rather than from rapid population growth, can generate patterns of demand that permit farmers in these areas to diversify out of staple cereal production and into higher value crop and animal products. It may also permit the release of some of the more fragile lands from crop production to less intensive forms of land use.

REFERENCES

Alchain, A.A., and H. Demsetz
   1973   The property rights paradigm. *Journal of Economic History* 33:16-77.

Ausubel, J., and H.E. Sladovich, eds.
   1989   *Technology and the Environment.* Washington, D.C.: National Academy Press.

Barnett, H.J., and C. Morse
   1963   *Scarcity and Growth: The Economics of Natural Resource Availability.* Baltimore: Johns Hopkins Press.

Batie, S.
   1989   Sustainable development: challenges to the profession of agricultural economics. *American Journal of Agricultural Economics* (December):1085-1101.

Binswanger, H.
   1974   A microeconomic approach to induced innovation. *Economic Journal* 84(December):940-958.
   1978   Induced technical change: evolution of thought. Pp. 13-43 in H.P. Binswanger and V.W. Ruttan, eds., *Induced Innovation: Technology Institutions and Development.* Baltimore: Johns Hopkins University Press.

Binswanger, H., and V.W. Ruttan, eds.
   1978   *Induced Innovation: Technology Institutions and Development.* Baltimore: Johns Hopkins University Press.

Boserup, E.
   1965   *The Conditions of Agricultural Growth: The Economics of Agrarian Change Under Population Pressure.* Chicago: Aldine.

Boyce, J.K.
   1987   *Agrarian Impasse in Bengal: Institutional Constraints to Technological Change.* Oxford: Oxford University Press.

Bromley, D.W.
   1989   *Economic Interests and Institutions: The Conceptual Foundations of Public Policy.* New York: Basil Blackwell.

Burmeister, L.L.
   1987   The South Korean green revolution: induced or directed innovation? *Economic Development and Cultural Change* 35:767-790.

Buttel, F.H.
   1988   *Agricultural Research and Development and the Appropriation of Progressive Symbols: Some Observations on the Politics of Ecological Agriculture.* Rural Sociology Bulletin No. 151. Ithaca, N.Y.: Cornell University.

Cleaver, H.M., Jr.
   1972   The contradiction of the green revolution. *American Economic Review* 62:177-186.

Commons, J.R.
   1950   *The Economics of Collective Action.* New York: MacMillan.

Cummings, R.W.
   1989   Modernizing Asia and the Near East: Agricultural Research in the 1990s. Mimeo.

Bureau for Science and Technology, U.S. Agency for International Development, Washington, D.C.

Daly, H.E.
1991 From empty world economics to full world economics: recognizing an historical turning point in economic development. Pp. 18-26 in R. Goodland, H. Daly, and S. El Serafy, eds., *Environmentally Sustainable Economic Development: Building on Bruntland*. Environment Working Paper No. 46. Washington, D.C.: World Bank.

Davis, L., and D.C. North
1971 *Institutional Change and American Economic Growth*. Cambridge, England: Cambridge University Press.

de Janvry, A.
1973 A socioeconomic model of induced innovation for Argentine agricultural development. *Quarterly Journal of Economics* 87(August):410-435.

Demsetz, H.
1967 Toward a theory of property rights. *American Economic Review* 57:347-359.

Douglass, G.K., ed.
1984 *Agricultural Sustainability in a Changing World Order*. Boulder, Colo.: Westview Press.

Edwards, C.
1988 Real prices received by farmers keep falling. *Choices* Fourth Quarter:22-23.

Feeny, D.
1982 *The Political Economy of Productivity: Thai Agricultural Development: 1880-1975*. Vancouver: University of British Columbia Press.

Field, A.J.
1981 The problem with neoclassical institutional economics: a critique with special reference to the North/Thomas model of pre-1500 Europe. *Explorations in Economic History* 18:174-198.

Goeller, H.E., and A.M. Weinberg
1976 The age of substitutability. *Science* 191(February 20): 683-689.

Goodland, R.
1991 The case that the world has reached limits. Pp. 5-17 in R. Goodland, H. Daly, and S. El Serafy, eds., *Environmentally Sustainable Economic Development: Building on Bruntland*. Environment Working Paper No. 46. Washington, D.C.: World Bank.

Graham-Tomasi, T.
1991 Sustainability: concepts and implications for agricultural research policy. Pp. 81-102 in P.G. Pardey, J. Roseboom, and J.R. Anderson, eds., *Agricultural Research Policy: International Quantitative Perspectives*. New York: Cambridge University Press.

Griffin, K.
1974 *The Political Economy of Agrarian Change: An Essay on the Green Revolution*. Cambridge, Mass.: Harvard University Press.

Groves, T., R. Radner, and S. Reiter, eds.
1987 *Information, Incentives and Economic Mechanisms*. Minneapolis: University of Minnesota Press.

Hayami, Y., and M. Kikuchi
1981 *Asian Village Economy at the Crossroads: An Economic Approach to Institutional Change*. Baltimore: Johns Hopkins University Press.

Hayami, Y., and V.W. Ruttan
1971 *Agricultural Development: An International Perspective*. Baltimore: Johns Hopkins University Press.

1985 *Agricultural Development: An International Perspective*, 2nd ed. Baltimore: Johns Hopkins University Press.
1987 Population growth and agricultural productivity. Pp. 57-104 in D. G. Johnson and R.D. Lee, eds., *Population Growth and Economic Development: Issues and Evidence*. Madison: University of Wisconsin Press.
1991 Rapid population growth and technical and institutional change. Pp. 127-157 in G. Tapinos, D. Blanchet, and D.E. Horlacher, eds., *Consequences of Rapid Population Growth in Developing Countries*. New York: Taylor and Francis.

Hurwicz, L.
1972 An informationally decentralized system. Pp. 297-333 in C.B. McGuire and R. Radner, eds., *Decision and Organization*. Amsterdam: North-Holland.

James, D.E., P. Nijkamp, and J.B. Opschoor
1989 Ecological sustainability in economic development. Pp. 27-48 in F. Archibugi and P. Nijkamp, eds., *Economy and Ecology: Toward Sustainable Development*. Dordrecht, The Netherlands: Kluwer Academic Publishers.

Kako, T.
1978 Decomposition analysis of derived demand for factor inputs: the case of rice production in Japan. *American Journal of Agricultural Economics* 60(November):628-635.

Kawagoe, T., K. Otsuka, and Y. Hayami
1986 Induced bias of technical change in agriculture: the United States and Japan, 1880-1990. *Journal of Political Economy* 3:523-544.

Kikuchi, M., and Y. Hayami
1978 Agricultural growth against a land resource constraint: a comparative history of Japan, Taiwan, Korea, and the Philippines. *Journal of Economic History* 38:839-864.

Knight, F.H.
1952 Institutionalism and empiricism in economics. *American Economic Review* 42(May):1951.

Koppel, B., and E. Oasa
1987 Induced innovation theory and Asian green revolution: a case study of ideology and neutrality. *Development and Change* 18:29-67.

Lee, R.D.
1980 A historical perspective on economic aspects of the population explosion: the case of pre-industrial England. Pp. 517-566 in R.H. Easterlin, ed., *Population and Economic Change in Developing Countries*. Chicago: University of Chicago Press.

Lipton, M.
1991 Accelerated Resource Degradation by Third World Agriculture: Created in the Commons, in the West, or in Bed. Paper presented at the Seminar on Agricultural Sustainability and Poverty Alleviation: Issues and Polices, Feldafing, Germany, Sept. 23-27.

Mikesell, R.F.
1991 Project evaluation and sustainable development. Pp. 54-60 in R. Goodland, H. Daly, and S. El Serafy, eds., *Environmentally Sustainable Economic Development: Building on Bruntland*. Environmental Working Paper 46. Washington, D.C.: World Bank.

National Research Council
1989 *Alternative Agriculture*. Committee on the Role of Alternative Farming Methods in Modern Production Agriculture, Board on Agriculture. Washington, D.C.: National Academy Press.

1990 *Research Strategies for the U.S. Global Change Research Program.* Committee on Global Change of the Commission on Geoscience, Environment and Resources. Washington, D.C.: National Academy Press.
1991 *Policy Implications of Greenhouse Warming.* Committee on Science, Engineering, and Public Policy. Washington, D.C.: National Academy Press.

Nghiep, L.
1979 The structure and changes of technology in pre-war Japanese agriculture. *American Journal of Agricultural Economics* 61(4):687-693.

Norgaard, R.B.
1991 *Sustainability as Intergenerational Equity: The Challenge to Economic Thought and Practice.* Washington, D.C.: World Bank.

North, D.C.
1983 A theory of economic change. Science 219(January 14):163-164.

North, D.C., and R.P. Thomas
1970 An economic theory of the rise of the western world. *Economic History Review* 23:1-17.

Olson, M.
1982 *The Rise and Decline of Nations: Economic Growth, Stagflation, and Social Rigidities.* New Haven: Yale University Press.

Parry, M.
1990 *Climate Change and World Agriculture.* London: Earthscan Publications.

Pearce, D.W., E. Barbier, and A. Makrandaya
1990 *Sustainable Development: Economics and Environment in the Third World.* Brookfield, V.T.: Gower.

Pingali, P.
1988 *Intensification and Diversification of Asian Rice Farming Systems.* Agricultural Economics Paper RR-41. Los Baños, Laguna, Philippines: International Rice Research Institute.

Pingali, P., Y. Bigot, and H. P. Binswanger
1987 *Agricultural Mechanization and the Evolution of Farming Systems in Sub-Saharan Africa.* Baltimore: Johns Hopkins University Press.

Plucknett, D.H., and N.J.H. Smith
1986 Sustaining agricultural yields. *BioScience* 36:40-45.

Pray, C.E.
1983 Private agricultural research in Asia. *Food Policy* (May):131-140.

President's Materials Policy Commission
1952 *Resources for Freedom.* Washington, D.C.: U.S. Government Printing Office.

President's Water Resources Policy Commission
1950 *A Water Policy for the American People,* Vol. 1. Washington, D.C.: U.S. Government Printing Office.

Pretty, J.N.
1990 Sustainable agriculture in the Middle Ages: the English manor. *Agricultural History Review* 3(1):1-19.

Price, C.
1991 Do high discount rates destroy tropical forests? *Journal of Agricultural Economics* 42(January):77-85.

Reilly, J., and R. Bucklin
1989 Climate change and agriculture. *World Agriculture Situation and Outlook Report.* Washington, D.C.: USDA/ARS, WAS-55:43-46.

Robinson, W.C., and W. Schutjer
1984 Agricultural development and demographic change: a generalization of the Boserup model. *Economic Development and Cultural Change* 32:355-366.

Rogoff, M.H., and S.L. Rawlins
   1987   Food security: a technological alternative. *BioScience* 37(December):800-807.
Runge, C.F.
   1981a Institutions and Common Property Externalities: The Assurance Problem in Economic Development. Unpublished Ph.D. dissertation, University of Wisconsin, Madison.
   1981b Common property externalities: isolation assurance and resource depletion in a traditional grazing context. *American Journal of Agricultural Economics* 63:595-606.
Ruttan, V.W.
   1971   Technology and the environment. *American Journal of Agricultural Economics* 53(December):707-717.
   1988a Cultural endowments and economic development: what can we learn from anthropology? *Economic Development and Cultural Change* 36(April):247-271.
   1988b Sustainability is not enough. *American Journal of Alternative Agriculture* 3(Spring/Summer):128-130.
Ruttan, V.W., ed.
   1989   *Biological and Technical Constraints on Crop and Animal Productivity: Report on a Dialogue.* St. Paul: University of Minnesota Department of Agricultural and Applied Economics.
   1992   *Sustainable Agriculture and the Environment: Perspectives on Growth and Constraints.* Boulder, Colo.: Westview Press.
Ruttan, V.W., and Y. Hayami
   1984   Toward a theory of induced institutional innovation. *Journal of Development Studies* 20(July):203-223.
Sanders, J.H., and V.W. Ruttan
   1978   Biased choice of technology in Brazilian agriculture. Pp. 276-296 in H.P. Binswanger and V.W. Ruttan, eds., *Induced Innovation: Technology, Institutions and Development.* Baltimore: Johns Hopkins University Press.
Sen, A.K.
   1967   Isolation, assurance and the social rate of discount. *Quarterly Journal of Economics* 81:112-124.
Solow, R.M.
   1974   The economics of resources or the resources of economics. *American Economic Review* 64(May):1-14.
   1991   Sustainability: Economists Perspective. Marine Policy Center, J. Seeward Johnson Lecture, Woods Hole Oceanographic Institution, Woods Hole, Mass., June 14.
Technical Advisory Committee/Consultative Group on International Agricultural Research (TAC/CGIAR)
   1989   *Sustainable Agricultural Production: Implications for International Research.* Rome: Food and Agriculture Organization of the United Nations.
Thirtle, C.G., and V.W. Ruttan
   1987   *The Role of Demand and Supply in the Generation and Diffusion of Technical Change.* London: Harwood Academic Publishers.
van Bath, S.H.S.
   1963   *The Agrarian History of Western Europe, A.D. 500-1850.* London: Edward Arnold.
Weir, D.
   1991   An historical perspective on the economic consequences of rapid population growth. Pp. 41-66 in G. Tapinos, D. Blanchet, and D.E. Horlacher, eds., *Consequences of Rapid Population Growth in Developing Countries.* New York: Taylor and Francis.
White, L.A.
   1974   Human culture. *Encyclopedia Brittanica*, Vol. 8, 15th ed. Chicago: Benton.

Whitehead, A.N.
    1925   *Science and the Modern World.* New York: Macmillan.
Wittfogel, K.A.
    1957   *Oriental Despotism: A Comparative Study of Total Power.* New Haven: Yale University Press.
World Commission on Environment and Development
    1987   *Our Common Future.* New York: Oxford University Press for The Bruntland Commission.

Appendix

Workshop Agenda

Thursday, December 5

9:00-9:15 a.m.	Welcome and rationale *Carole L. Jolly*, Committee on Population *Barbara Boyle Torrey*, Committee on Population and Population Reference Bureau
9:15-10:15	Historical Overview of Land Use Change *M. Gordon Wolman*, Department of Geography and Environmental Engineering, Johns Hopkins University
10:15-11:15	Measurement of Land Use Change *Isaak S. Zonneveld*, International Institute of Aerospace Survey and Earth Sciences, The Netherlands
11:15-11:45	Break
11:45-12:45 p.m.	Current Approaches to the Study of Population Change and Land Use: Correlations and the Research Efforts of Other Organizations *Billie L. Turner II*, George Perkins Marsh Institute, Graduate School of Geography, Clark University

12:45-1:45	Lunch
1:45-2:45	Population Growth and Technological Change in Agriculture *Hans Binswanger*, Agriculture Operations, Latin America and the Caribbean, The World Bank
2:45-3:45	Using Cross-National Data to Understand Population, Land Use, and the Environment *Richard E. Bilsborrow*, Carolina Population Center, University of North Carolina at Chapel Hill
3:45-4:15	Break
4:15-5:15	Discussant *Steward T.A. Pickett*, Institute of Ecosystem Studies, The New York Botanical Garden

Friday, December 6

Case Studies

8:30-10:00 a.m.	Africa *Uma Lele*, Food and Resource Economics Department, University of Florida Nigeria *Michael Mortimore*, University of Cambridge
10:00-10:30	Break
10:30-12:45 p.m.	India—Analytical Strategies for Studying Population Change and Land Use *Robert E. Evenson*, Department of Economics, Yale University Mauritius *Wolfgang Lutz*, Population Program, International Institute for Applied Systems Analysis, Austria

	Thailand *Theodore Panayotou*, Harvard Institute for International Development and Department of Economics, Harvard University (Advisor to the Natural Resources and Environment Division of the Thailand Development Research Institute)
12:45-1:45	Lunch
1:45-2:30	Honduras *Billie R. DeWalt*, Department of Anthropology, University of Kentucky*
2:30-3:30	Population Growth, Environmental Change, and Institutional Innovation *Vernon W. Ruttan*, Department of Agricultural and Applied Economics, University of Minnesota
3:30-4:00	Break
4:00-5:00	Wrap-up and discussion *Samuel H. Preston*, Committee on Population and Population Studies Center, University of Pennsylvania

---

*Now, Graduate School of Public and International Affairs and the Center for Latin American Studies, University of Pittsburgh